IDENTITY POLITICS AND ITS **IMPACT** ON THE **SPREAD** OF **DIGITAL MARKETING**

(A Framework to Manage Country Level Political Risk in Ethiopia)

DANIEL B. SOLOMON

BALBOA.PRESS

A DIVISION OF HAY HOUSE

Balboa Press books may be ordered through booksellers or by contacting:

Balboa Press
A Division of Hay House
1663 Liberty Drive
Bloomington, IN 47403
www.balboapress.com
844-682-1282

Because of the dynamic nature of the Internet, any web addresses or links contained in this book may have changed since publication and may no longer be valid. The views expressed in this work are solely those of the author and do not necessarily reflect the views of the publisher, and the publisher hereby disclaims any responsibility for them.

The author of this book does not dispense medical advice or prescribe the use of any technique as a form of treatment for physical, emotional, or medical problems without the advice of a physician, either directly or indirectly. The intent of the author is only to offer information of a general nature to help you in your quest for emotional and spiritual well-being. In the event you use any of the information in this book for yourself, which is your constitutional right, the author and the publisher assume no responsibility for your actions.

Any people depicted in stock imagery provided by Getty Images are models, and such images are being used for illustrative purposes only.
Certain stock imagery © Getty Images.

Print information available on the last page.

ISBN: 978-1-9822-7224-1 (sc)
ISBN: 978-1-9822-7223-4 (e)

Balboa Press rev. date: 07/29/2021

Contents

Figures and Tables

Glossary of Abbreviations

ADP	Amhara Democratic Party
EDF	Ethiopian Defense Force
EICTDA	Ethiopian Information and Communication Technology Development Agency
EPRDF	Ethiopian People's Revolutionary Democratic Front
ETA	Ethiopian Telecommunication Agency
ETC	Ethiopia Telecommunications Corporation
ICT	Information and Communications Technology
IM	Instant Message
LLC	Limited Liability Company
MCIT	Ministry of Communications and Information Technology
NGO	Nongovernmental organization
NISS	National Intelligence and Security Services
ODP	Oromo Democratic Party
PID	Project Information Document
PP	Prosperity Parity
SMS	Short Message Service
SEPDM	Southern Ethiopian People's Democratic Movement
TPLF	Tigrayan People's Liberation Front
VA	Virginia
VOA	Voice of America
VoIP	Voice over Internet Protocol
WTO	World Trade Organization

Dedication

THIS RESEARCH BOOK IS DEDICATED to my biological father, Solomon Beyene Gizaw, and my sister Birkinesh Solomon Beyene.

Acknowledgment

THIS RESEARCH OWES MULTIPLE DEBTS to many relatives, friends, and colleagues. The first that comes into the picture is my mother, the late Bizunesh Bekele Cheregn. She has always been the consistent source of my support, encouragement, and courage since I have been living. Her wishes, inspirations, and legacies have instituted the rooftop of my self-attainment. I have learned all the skills it took me to successfully navigate through the ups and downs of life in this brief but most challenging world.

She was my guru, coach, and mentor. She has thought me the truth in love and a great prospect. She has carried me in her womb, back, and heart until she had been alive among us. Now she is no more with us in this corporal world, but she lives in my heart until my breath turns to air.

In short, all my success today is just because of her. As a caring and loving mother, she has always been a special gift to me, the most invaluable gift from God above. May all the credits and honors this work goes to her. I also dedicate this dissertation to her.

Likewise, my deepest gratitude goes to Mr. Solomon Beyene Gizaw, my biological father, whom I have not known until I have lived half of my lifetime. As to my life principle, a father is as a thoughtful matter as life itself. He is the author of the life of his children. He begins their beginnings in the womb of the mother. Life comes from him while the mother builds up the body. That is why we all take our respective father's names next to ours.

I am not questioning my mother for not letting me know the seed I grew from into such a big tree. I know her inside out. Conceivably, she must have a good reason not to do so. However, from the stories, she had been telling me, I was able to apprehend her deep love and affection for my father, who still carries her in his loving heart. Not to say life is prejudicial, despite their bottomless love, nature rebutted them a life together even after I was conceived in the heart and womb of my mother.

In the end, nature revealed the truth. Somewhere in the Bible, there is a verse that says "For those who love God and are called according to his will, everything works out for good." It is true. Everything works out for good. Though happened in the absence of my mother, the synthetic gash between me and my father has lastly turned out to be for our benefit.

Eventually, I got to know my loving and caring father, who appears to look alike a lot with me apart from the effect of aging on his side. Yes, we look alike as if we are identical twins, more so replicas. At times, I think as if my body is like his retention mound.

Be that as it may, my gorgeous father has encouraged me enough, even in his absence. The desire of his spirit has helped me to keep going and straight. I have always been persistent amidst encounters and challenges. His absence had made him louder than what he would have been in his presence.

His inherited genes and endowed talents and pearls of wisdom are all stowed across my body. In short, he has always been supportive in translating my thoughts into digestible substances, all the way since my birth, and even so, into this date. Hence, his considerations and thoughts, have been echoed even in this specific research work.

I am also deeply indebted to my wife Sara Solomon. We have recently celebrated our 25th year of martial anniversary with our three wonderfully and fearfully created boys and my most adoring biological father and most loving sister. My sons have been a pleasure in my life. They are continuous sustenance to all my endeavors in life.

It is a privilege to be a father of such blessing boys. A good sense of truth is always ahead of them, leading them all in their ways. It is inspiring, cheering, and even encouraging to have them in my life. At times, I take them as the source of my contentment. Their presence makes me happy. They give meaning and perspective to my life. In the face of the various storms and trials, they have always been the basis of my strength.

I cannot afford to pass by the support I have gotten from my beloved sister, Birkinesh Solomon, and her God-given husband, Ephrem Tsegaye. If truth be told, they are the latter-day blessings of my life. I take them as a divine gift, a gift from God above. I am very much blessed by them coming as favors in my family. They are the true troopers that I have known in the spiritual realm, them setting good examples to follow and a wonderful testimony to abide by.

They know how to make their cases before the Most High and get it done with all the faith packed in the core of their hearts. These are two loving couples united in marriage but have already made it together and one deep in their souls. Hence, their prayer can move mountains if they mean it to, for they have that strong unity that can shake the earth if given a place to stand on.

I am very much thankful to several friends and colleges who have helped me have a more profound sense of the subject matter of this research through their feedback and comment. Their inputs and contributions are incontestably inordinate. This research, however, expresses findings achieved in a scientific manner and procedures having been through due process. It doesn't necessarily echo my personal views. Nor does it tone the opinions and outlooks of those colleagues whose opinions helped in expanding the gist of the study at the very start.

I am also obliged to all who provided me their respective feedback on the initial idea of the study. I am also indebted to those who read through the draft copies of this paper and provided me a detailed comment as the research work advanced. I am appreciative to Mr. Wedajeneh Cherinet, Mr. Raj Varma, Mr. Ani Duta, Ms. Hargewoyin Meresha, Mr. Workiye Eshete, Mr. Abebe Berbere, Worku Yimmer (Ph.D.), Mr. Mesfin Kassa, Mr. Cyrus Hailu, Mr. Endalkachew Dotti, and Mr. Abas Ahimed for their good words, encouragements, and councils through this research endeavor.

The research has also received generous financial support in the form of grants from Dan Technology Consultant LLC, located at 2639 Memorial St Alexandria VA 22306. This company is founded on the 1st date of January 2019 and led by the researcher himself. Currently, it is tremendously contributing to validation, verification, software development, testing, and automation, here in the USA. Though it is a young and growing company, it was able to support the research. Therefore, I am obliged and appreciative.

The technical support, the professional advice, and the collaboration I got from the LIGS university professors, scholars, and entire staff throughout this research has been irreplaceable. I am especially indebted to Professor George Alexander, my academic advisor, who assisted me in the entire process of conducting and writing up this dissertation.

He was my closest educational mentor who has technically led me through the complete procedure during this practical journey. I would say he has been reassuring and inspiring me. Yet, he had a special way of pushing me to make this great project a reality.

Foreword

THIS IS A RESEARCH PAPER submitted to LIGS university in partial fulminant of a Ph.D. degree in Digital project management in 2020. The research was supervised and approved by Prof. George Alexander. Since the paper deals with a country-level political risk prevailing in the contemporary Ethiopia, publishing it might help the concerned stakeholders to take due course of action before things go out of hand subjecting the country to political mess and defragmentation.

As well known, poverty, drought, political repression, displacements, and goaded slaughter have been some of the major concerns impacting the economic growth and the political mesosphere of modern-day Ethiopia, at least, for the last three decades (Ethiopia: General Information, 2014). On top of that, the racial political order that the country has betrothed with since the Ethiopian People's Revolutionary Democratic Front (EPRDF), an ethnic federalist consisted of four political parties; namely Tigray People's Liberation Front (TPLF), Amhara Democratic Party (ADP), Oromo Democratic Party (ODP) and Southern Ethiopian People's Democratic Movement (SEPDM), came to office by grappling gun in contradiction of the then military junta at the beginning of the 1990s, has accosted the nation at the threshold of disintegration and fragmentation (Woldemariam, 2019) and (Lefort, 2018).

Since then, a sense of political and economic sidelining based on ethnic profile along with bad governance, government-supported corruption, miss-use of power, dearth of justice, and lack of the rule of law have attended a full-sized growth among the various ethnic groups in Ethiopia, with violent outbreaks raising several questions demanding impartiality, rule of law, constitutional reform and the likes.

Political turmoil, social disorder, ethnic cleansing, displacement, and street murder have become a sort of reoccurring incidents in most of the country with a higher concreteness in the Amhara and Oromia regional states. Certain evidence exhibit the fact that the majority of such human right abuses have been piloted by TPLF buoyed by the Egyptian regime that has a vested interest on the unrest of the country due to the Nile politics.

The regime has increasingly resorted to Internet shutdowns in times of crisis, arguing it is compulsory for public safety and curbing the spread of distorted information over the Internet. Nonetheless, such comprehensive actions are more like collective chastisement than a tactical response to public resistance.

It goes without saying that when the Internet is off, people's ability to express themselves is spontaneously limited, the economy suffers, citizens struggle to upload photos and videos documenting government overreach and abuse, students are cut off from their lessons, of all digital marketing suffers the most (Roth, 2020).

Although the regime commands the blackouts, it is the state-owned EthioTelecom, which is the sole Internet service provider in the country that implements the embargo. It chunks the entire Internet service, specific social media, certain messaging applications, and/or prevents any Internet traffic to live streaming platforms all over the nation or in some selected places so that the general public is unable to interconnect across the board.

What is more, even when the Internet remains available, at times there is a spectrum of overbroad rules and regulations that allow the government to pressure journalists, activities, and the general public from using the Internet profusely the way they need it. Above and beyond, investment in expanding the Internet and advancement of technology is controlled by the regime. Private investments are politically banned and frantically discouraged from participating in such endeavors.

Connecting all these dots, the researcher has a judicious concern and, thus, undertakes the alarm that the country might be subject to the digital divide in a few years provided that it doesn't change its political apparatuses from identity to idea based political spectrum. Apart from all other aftermaths of such a divide, the growth of digital marketing all over the country will not only be impeded but will be congested. Therefore, the researcher believes, it is worth doing such an academic study to find out if this concern is significantly valid and if it is, to recommend what might be done to reverse the course and moderate its impact to a substantial level.

The gist of this research is based on the assumption that identity-based politics could put the country into a sort of an in-house mess and chaos that might, in turn, reflect overwhelmingly into its external and global economic affiliation with the rest of the world. Recovering from this damage may be very expensive. Hence, this research is a kind of cautionary doorbell to the country to look profoundly take due action to reverse the course of the identity politics running the nation.

Abstract

DIGITAL MARKETING HAS A SUBSTANTIAL impact on economic growth. A public passion is essential for sustaining effective digital marketing. Identity politics shrinks the said passion for digital marketing. It also paves the way for a digital divide. The research concentrates on Ethiopia, a country that has been suffering from identity politics for the last three sold decades since EPRDF assumed office in 1991 through armed struggle against the then military junta. The study hypothesizes that by impacting public passion for digital marketing and paving the way to the digital divide, identity politics could establish a country-level political risk for a developing country like Ethiopia. The research analyzes the subsequent four questions. 1) Is there any significant relationship between identity politics and public passion for digital marketing? 2) Can identity politics lead to a digital divide when public passion for digital marketing diminishes? 3) Can identity politics establish a cautery level political risk in developing countries such as Ethiopia? 4) What kind of risk management framework would best help such countries to reverse the course of the problem? The researcher has reviewed scholarly reports, study materials, books, and other relevant literature. The sample size population contains 45 informants. All of them live in Addis Ababa, Ethiopia. The primary data was collected from the sample size population through questionnaires, focused group discussions, and interviews. The data was comprehensively analyzed using GPower and JAMOVIA. The finding exhibits that there is a significant association between identity politics and public passion for digital marketing. The digital divide has a probability of 7.8% to occur, given the said passion shrinks as an aftermath of identity politics. Eventually, the research suggests a concise risk management model that would help manage the crises.

Keywords: Country-level risk, digital business, digital divide, digital marketing, e-commerce, identity politics, internet availability, internet penetration, public passion for digital marketing, web trade.

Chapter One
INTRODUCTION

THE SHIFT FROM ANALOG TO digital technology and the extensive economic and social changes have not yet run their course. Instead, it continues, transforming the way business is run, production is structured, countries and firms trade, and people work and communicate. It is recasting the relationships between customers, workers, and employers. For instance, the present-day consumer is gradually moving towards a more digital marketing preference than the accustomed in-person shopping (Zimmerman, 2017).

Different customers have various motives for the migration. Kassa (2019), for instance, thinks that customers are moving to digital marketing largely because it is a click away and easy to do it[1]. Hailu (2019), on the other hand, believes that shopping in persons is becoming risky due to the prevalence of COVID 19 and therefore people tend to go online to do their shopping[2]. According to Gutema (2019), her friends prefer buying and sailing digitally online for a couple of reasons. First off, it is time and cost-effective. Secondly, there are vast varieties of products to choose from[3].

---

[1] Mesfin Kassa (September 05, 2019), Online Customers Market Preference, Interview by Daniel Solomon

[2] Cyrus Hailu (September 06, 2019), Online Customers Market Preference, Interview by Daniel Solomon

[3] Meaza Gutema (September 07, 2019), Online Customers Market Preference, Interview by Daniel Solomon

The migration has helped rising the number of customers shooing online. Some reports indicate that amazon, an American electronic commerce company, holds over 244 million customers worldwide (Kline, 2020). Similarly, eBay, a popular online open market, has attracted 180 million users in the last twenty-five years (Lin, 2020). The number of people buying goods and services online is close to 1.8 billion (Maryam, 2020).

Two major factors have contributed to achieving this vast number of customers in a short period. To begin with, customers like searching for products and making purchases from the comfort of their homes. A study conducted by Brief (2018) indicates that the vast majority (87%) of shoppers begin product searches on digital channels[4]. Shopping online has become a common practice among millions of people around the world (Kingsnorth, Digital Marketing Strategy: An Integrated Approach to Online Marketing, 2019). The instantaneous prevalence of coronavirus as a global pandemic has made digital marketing even a matter of necessity, not a choice due to the stay-home policies under practice worldwide.

Then, the very nature of digital marketing by itself is an attractive endeavor for online sellers and buyers. Besides, the immense potential of searching for an enormous number of products online and the real-time communication with clients are some of the benefits of digital marketing for several reasons (Hoover, 2019). First, it encompasses an extensive range of customers. Second, it has comparatively a very vast and enormous market.

---

[4] Dive Brief (2018), 87% of shoppers now begin product searches online, Retail Dive, https://www.retaildive.com /news/ 87-of-shoppers-now-begin-product-searches-online/530139/

Third, it increases sales volumes in significant size (Diamond, 2018). Fourth, rating a high level of customer satisfaction can transform the way the business engages clients (Deiss, Digital Marketing For Dummies, 2nd Edition, 2018). Sixth, it is the most efficient, accurate, and cost-effective way of marketing for both sides, buyers, and sellers (Kingsnorth, Digital Marketing Strategy: An Integrated Approach to Online Marketing, 2019). Finally, it is a measurable, computable, and scalable form of marketing.

Besides, a business can take advantage of digital consumer response to products, prices, qualities, events, trends, topics, and technologies (Ryan, 2019). In this regard, social media marketing is a popular tactic that allows businesses to be part of the online conversation with their customers about their products and other business matters[5]. Using these Media digital marketing provides a more tailored experience over shared video ads and custom-made goods (Beckwith, 2019).

The digital market has its way to track the achievement of the market, which helps find out what is working and what is not concerning the quality of the product, and price affordability, and other marketing-related matters (Jiwa, Marketing: A Love Story: How to Matter to Your Customers, 2016). Besides, it offers a substantial return on small investments (Saini, 2018).

The digital market is neither intrusive, nor interruptive, and yet it has better exposure, with greater engagement of customers from their respective comfort areas (Sherman, 2019). To sum up, digital marketing is exceedingly effective and can easily contribute to economic growth, by generating jobs, producing

---

[5] Mesfin Kassa (September 05, 2019), Online Customers Market Preference, Interview by Daniel Solomon

business opportunities, and creating platforms for people to exchange skills and experiences across the globe[6].

Despite the mentioned benefits, digital marketing is proportionally practiced by different states in the world. Countries with favorable political ideology, such as the USA, Canada, and European states, and Southeast Asian countries such as Japan and Korea have widely implemented digital marketing. Most of these countries have Internet penetration higher than 80% with more than 50 % smartphone users (Varghese, 2017). In short, the favorable political ideology in these counties has created an opportunity for citizens to do digital marketing platforms and market their products worldwide.

On the contrary, developing countries like Libya, Sudan, Somalia, and Ethiopia, which are stressed with perplexing internal contentions due to identity political activities, do not seem to be ready for digital marketing opportunities (Reda, 2018). The first two of these countries are labeled failed states (Engel, 2016) and (Ghaith Shennib, 2018).

The outstanding two might be labeled the same soon if they do not consider a political shift from identity to idea-based politics[7]. The government of a failed state is incapable to have good control of its people or resources, and there are very few, if any, public services such as the Internet (Failed Stats, 2021).

Ethiopia is one of these nations fast approaching the edge of a failed state status. It is sternly struggling with deeply rooted identity politics instigating the death and persecution

---

[6] Meaza Gutema (September 07, 2019), Online Customers Market Preference, Interview by Daniel Solomon
[7] Solomon Gizaw (January 10, 2020), Identity Politics and Its Impact on Public Passion for Digital Marketing, Interview by Daniel Solomon

of citizens in thousands[8]. The government is unable to protect citizens in certain places within its territory (Gedamu, 2018). According to Hailu (2019) identify polities is the root cause for the mess shaking the country inside-out[9]. Shortage of hard currencies, the dearth of appropriate legal outlines and order, the prevalence of war, ethnic cleansing, and mass arrest resulting from inadequate penetration of the Internet are all emanating from the same source, identity politics[10].

In other words, the government structure is utterly ineffective. As a result, it deliberately keeps the country offline by imposing consistent Internet outages[11]. In addition, the government does consider digital marketing as a macro industry and a job creation endeavor[12].

As per the findings of this research, there is very poor availability of the Internet in Ethiopia. Only 17.8% of the entire population had access to the Internet at the end of 2019 (Internet World Status, 2019). In that same year, according to this same report, the Facebook users in the country represent only 5.8% of the population. Such poor coverage of the Internet has to do with identity politics that has disintegrated the country in two several regional states based on ethnic profiles of citizens.

Most of the African countries have already observed identity politics as malicious and put a law in place that prohibits the

---

[8] Hargewoyin Marsha (January 12, 2020), Identity Politics and Its Impact on Public Passion for Digital Marketing, Interview by Daniel Solomon
[9] Cyrus Hailu (September 06, 2019), Identity Politics and Its Impact on Public Passion for Digital Marketing, Interview by Daniel Solomon
[10] Solomon Gizaw (January 10, 2020), Identity Politics and Its Impact on Public Passion for Digital Marketing, Interview by Daniel Solomon
[11] Cyrus Hailu (September 06, 2019), Identity Politics and Its Impact on Public Passion for Digital Marketing, Interview by Daniel Solomon
[12] Hargewoyin Marsha (January 12, 2020), Identity Politics and Its Impact on Public Passion for Digital Marketing, Interview by Daniel Solomon

act of politically mobilizing the public based on such political creed (Lovise, The politics of ethnicity in Ethiopia: Actors. power and mobilization under ethnic federalism, 2011). Nearly in all these African countries, the use of ethnic differences as an explicit basis for political representation has been overruled by law. Hence, they have maintained reasonably better political stability and less internal conflict. In return, they have built comparatively a better atmosphere for digital marketing to progress in their respective countries.

Conversely, Ethiopia, since 1991, has viciously imposed a deteriorating system of ethnic-based federalism that compromises the sovereignty and independence of the country and offers each ethnic group the right of self-determination, setting the civic rights of the public notwithstanding (Turton, 2016).

This has made the self-ruling nation feel and look like a state established by seemingly other smaller self-governing countries in the form of coming together federation, while it had to be a holding together federation since none of the regional states had had a record of being a sovereign country in their respective account of history.

Even though, the intention of the coming together federation was to accommodate ethnic diversity, this act of reinventing the country based on identity politics has cost the citizens the worst of scrapes[13]. There were quite a significant number of reports coming out exposing these scraps and predicaments.

Some of these reports were from non-state wrought media and human rights reports on ethnic conflict, ethnic cleansing, and brutal mass murder at various times (Taye D. B., 2017). Be that as it may, the political canon enforced as a legal framework

---

[13] Cyrus Hailu (September 06, 2019), Identity Politics and Its Impact on Public Passion for Digital Marketing, Interview by Daniel Solomon

for ethnic-based federalism in the form of a constitution is still operational opening the gate for disintegration if any of the states would prefer to go astray.

The legal framework has dismembered the country into nine regional states in such a way that it favors identity-based politics (Mamdani, 2019). Sidama has recently been announced as the tenth regional state of Ethiopia by The National Electoral Board of Ethiopia (NEBE) on the 23rd date of November 2019 (Demissie, 2019).

More claims and petitions are coming up from several other ethnic groups suggesting a somber appeal for a greater devolution of power within the South Nations and Nationalities, which clenches well over fifty different ethnic groups that have their typical languages, cultures, philosophies, and beliefs (Matfess, 2019).

On top of all these, the tendency with TPLF does not sound right. Its intact legal alliance and synchronization with the central government have been vanishing since Prime Minister Abiy Ahmed has disbanded EPRDF and replaced it with PP, to renovate and transform the politics of the nation (Gardner, 2020). Their difference could not be arrested thru discussions and negations around a table. Instead, it got blown to a full-scale war where thousands have been killed from both sides[14].

The war began on the 4th of November 2021 with the TPLF attack on the Northern Command bases and headquarters of the Ethiopian National Defense Force (ENDF) in the Tigray Region (Nagy, 2020). This is just one example of the outcome of identity-based politics, can do to a nation. It cannot be handled thru a peaceful discussion around a table. This is so

---

[14] Hargewoyin Marsha (January 12, 2020), Identity Politics and Its Impact on Public Passion for Digital Marketing, Interview by Daniel Solomon

because the difference between the two parties originates from identity, no idea[15]. In short, identity politics do not have room for discussion. It is not open to the democratic effort. It always considers the other party as an adversary[16].

This research examined the impact of the practice of identity politics on the public passion for digital marketing. It has also investigated the probability of the occurrence of the digital divide as an aftermath of identity politics. The outcome indicated that identity politics has a significant relationship with public passion.

There is also a 7.8% probability for the digital divide to transpire if the stakeholders do not take proper actions to move from identity to idea-based politics. Hence, identity-based politics is a country-level risk for the existence of Ethiopia as a nation. The research recommends a risk management framework that would help the country mitigate the risk.

1.1. Structure and Content of the Research

There are five major chapters under this research. The first chapter embraces nine subtopics. First four subparts deliberate on the structure of the research, the background of the study area, the purpose of the study, and the research questions. Then, the subsequent three subtopics discuss the assumptions and hypotheses of the research, along with the statement of the problem, and the scope of the study. The outstanding two address the significance of the study coupled with some of the limitations of the study.

The second chapter is much about the review of related

---

[15] Solomon Gizaw (January 10, 2020), Identity Politics and Its Impact on Public Passion for Digital Marketing, Interview by Daniel Solomon
[16] Sara Solomon (January 12, 2020), Identity Politics and Its Impact on Public Passion for Digital Marketing, Interview by Daniel Solomon

literature. It has ten parts under it. Historical milestones in Ethiopian politics, identity politics in Ethiopia, and the advancement of technology and digital marketing are the first three subtopics discoursed in the chapter. Then, Internet availability in Ethiopia, Internet impact on world politics, Internet impact on Ethiopian politics, and Internet Impact on Ethiopian economy is briefly touched upon. The final three topics under the review of related literature comprise digital divide essence and occurrence, risk management framework, and theoretical framework.

In this chapter, academic journals, proceedings, pertain books, documents are reviewed. Besides, the prevailing best industry practices, the observation of the researcher, and the feedback gathered from the informants of the research have been discussed. Eventually, a theoretical framework is molded. This framework has given shape and perspective to the entire gist of the research and its findings.

The third chapter considers the methodology used in the research work. It discusses how the research data was collected, where it is collected from, the different types of data that was collected, and when was it collected. It also talks about the demography of the informants, what methods and tools were used to collect the data, and how the data is analyzed and scrutinized. The chapter addresses the steadiness, dependability, and credibility of the research data. It also describes the depth of its coverage and appropriateness to conduct academic research at this level.

Chapter four discusses the findings captured from the analysis of the data. The discussion embraces a total of five parts. The first part handles demography-related findings. The second part parleys about the academic standards and income levels of the informants. The third part is about the impact of identity politics on the public passion for digital marketing and the prospect of the digital divide in Ethiopia.

In the end, there is a brief conclusion that summarizes the findings of the research. In this section, proper recommendations and suggestions have also been proposed to all concerned parties and stakeholders. The study is supported by graphs, charts, tables. Related references and footnotes are enclosed at the end of the research work. What is more, a list of acronyms used in the research paper, the questionnaire, the focused group discussion, and interview questions are appended towards the end.

1.2. Background to the Study Area

Ethiopia, the cradle of humanity (Hadingham, 2015), the mother of ancient civilization (Jaide, 2007), and the symbol of the freedom of the black man (Mulugeta, 2017), currently referred to as, the Federal Democratic Republic of Ethiopia, is located in the Horn of Africa. Second, to Nigeria which has 181, 563,000 citizens, Ethiopia is the most populated African 10th biggest country with an estimated population of 117.001, 959 million (Ethiopia Population Live, 2021), of which more than 84 percent are estimated to live in rural areas.

Ethiopia is a landlocked nation divided into by the great rift valley. The country covers 1,119,683 square kilometers. It is adjoined by Eritrea to the north, Djibouti to the northeast, Somalia to the east, Kenya to the south, and Sudan to the west. It covers a sum of 1.13 million sq. km which is about 437,794 sq. miles (Ethiopia country profile, 2018). The country is the place of origin for the coffee (Arabica) bean and is sometimes referred to as the land of natural contrasts, home to vast fertile West, jungles, and numerous rivers, and the world's hottest settlement of Dallol in its North.

Ethiopia has been under the monarchic rule and the communist military junta for years (Hunter, 2014), before falling into the hands of EPRDF, the then Ethiopian People's Revolutionary Democratic Front, which has finally evolved into PP, Prosperity Party, at the beginning of the 1990s. The contemporary government was established by PP recently in 2018 with the coming of Prime Minster Abiy Ahmed, who came up with a political credo called coming together.

The country, which has been passing through quite an extended and perplexing form of transformation, is a federal parliamentary republic, whereby the Prime Minister is the head of the nation. Ethiopia is believed to be the oldest independent country in Africa with a history of over 3000 years of civilization and governmental structure and yet politically one of the most unsteady states in the continent (MT, 2019).

The country is founded like an evolving country by the nations, nationalities, and peoples that are recuperated under nine states, recently one more region is added, which seem to have their citizens because of their respective ethnic profiles (Constitute, 2018). The states include Tigray, Afar, Amhara, Oromia, Somali, Benishangul-Gumuz, Southern Nations Nationalities and People Region (SNNPR), Gambella and Harari, and the recent Sidama. There are also two administrative states Addis Ababa City administration and the Dire Dawa city council. These regional states and the two cities are further divided into eight hundred woredas and around 15,000 kebeles.

The major ethnic groups embrace Oromo 34.4%, Amhara (Amara) 27%, Somali (Somalie) 6.2%, Tigray (Tigrinya) 6.1%, Sidama 4%, Gurage 2.5%, Welaita 2.3%, Hadiya 1.7%, Afar (Affar) 1.7%, Gamo 1.5%, Gedeo 1.3%, Silte 1.3%, Kefficho 1.2%, other 8.8% (world C. o., 2019). In terms of religion, according to this report (world C. o., 2019), the current population of Ethiopia is distributed as Orthodox 43.5%, Muslim 33.9%, Protestant 18.5%, traditional 2.7%, Catholic 0.7%, other 0.6% (Lewis, 2018).

Agriculture is the mainstay of the Ethiopian economy involving the major source of employment and gross national product. More than 80% of the population lives in rural areas (world C. o., 2019). Agriculture contributing 41.4% of the country's gross domestic product (GDP), 83.9% of the total exports, and 80% of all employment in the country Infant child, and maternal mortality have fallen sharply over the past decade, but the total fertility rate has declined more slowly, and the population continues to grow (Mundi, 2017).

The rising age of marriage and the increasing proportion of women remaining single have contributed to fertility reduction (Family Planning Program In Ethiopia Health And Social Care Essay, 2016). While the use of modern contraceptive methods among married women has increased significantly from 6 percent in 2000 to 27 percent in 2012, the overall rate is still quite low (Tekelab, 2015). All said, Ethiopia's rapid population growth is putting increasing pressure on land resources, expanding environmental degradation, and raising vulnerability to food shortages (Feyisa, 2017).

Following this internal confrontation coupled with the tensions between Ethiopia and Sudan over the disputed al-Fashqa area, some political analysts have a strong fear that this war could escalate further, leading to the disintegration of the country, which would have significant economic and political repercussions for all countries in the Horn of Africa. The impact of this war on the availability of the Internet, and by so doing on digital marketing and other online activities are so somber.

On top of the poor Internet coverage and Facebook penetration in the country, the government keeps blocking the Internet for political reasons such as concealing the aftermath of the aforesaid war, mass massacres, and enormous displacements caused by identity politics (Babatunde, 2016). Needless to mention, such acts of governmental violations worsen the condition. Leave alone doing digital marketing online, accessing basic information such as daily news, reports and political analysis would be a back-breaking task to the very small percentage of the population that has access to the internet (Tobor, 2017). Therefore, despite the passion of the citizens for digital marketing, the opportunity to practice the same seems to be limited or constrained.

To draw a better picture of the situation, if we compare Ethiopia with its adjacent but in a relative term civically steady and stable country Kenya, Ethiopia seems to perform at a very regressive juncture in the area (Country comparison Ethiopia vs Kenya, 2019). Among many other facts, this can exhibit vividly how the dearth of democracy and steady political atmosphere desperately influence the growth of social media along with digital marketing and all other internet-related deals. As a matter of fact, in Kenya, 83% of the population has access to the internet, and 63% of them have subscribed to Facebook (Social Media Stats Kenya, 2019).

With more than 40 percent of the population below the age of 15 and a fertility rate of over 5 children per woman and even higher in rural areas (Worldmeters, 2019), Ethiopia will have to make further progress in meeting its family planning needs if it is to achieve the age structure necessary for reaping a demographic dividend in the coming decades (Mundi, 2017).

It is eminent that Ethiopia is home to the African Union and plays an influential role in mediating African conflicts. Ethiopia was a founding member of the Common Market for Eastern and Southern Africa (COMESA) (Ethiopia: General Information, 2014). The latest estimate of internet usage is 16,437,811 and internet penetration is about 12% (Internet Users Statistics for Africa, 2017).

The report indicates that until recently only 14.9% of Ethiopians have access to the internet of them 4.1% have subscribed to Facebook (Group, 2019). What is more, whenever political fierceness and violence flares in the country, Ethiopia continues to turn off the internet without any kind of rule of law (Solomon, VOA News, 2018).

Dozens of people have died in ethnic clashes in September 2018 on the outskirts of Ethiopia's capital, Addis Ababa (Solomon, VOA News, 2018). In that same month, other 23 people were killed in a weekend of violence targeting the capital Addis Ababa (Maasho, 2018). A couple of years back, other 80 people have been killed in Ethiopia amid an outbreak of ethnic unrest (Pilling, 2018). Recently 239 people were murdered from protests and ethnic violence that erupted in Ethiopia following the murder of a popular singer from the Oromo ethnic group (Corey, 2020). As protesters continued to remonstrate taking the issue to the streets in opposition to EPRDF, to handle the situation, the government turned off the internet for weeks. This is not a one-time incident.

At present, the federal government in Ethiopia has been overwhelmed by seemingly internal warfare with the Tigray region, the war between regional forces and the Ethiopian federal army began. Though, this war has been pronounced to have come to an end by the federal government, still are some indications that exhibit the fact that the war is in progress around the bush. Some wanted officials are not yet arrested, there are caves and pushes under the full control of the ex-government of the Tigray region.

1.3. Statement of the Problem

Ethiopia is one of the world's most ethnically heterogeneous societies (Calhoun, 1999). Until recently, the political, social, and economic dominancy of specific ethnic groups, mainly the Amhara and Tigre populations, have played a major role in shaping the country's geopolitical social and historical aspects as an aggregated and integrated nation (Belay, 2016). Nonetheless, after EPRDF took office in 1991 and introduced this identity politics, it has been engaged in a disguised scheme of annoying the national unity by propagating revulsion and animosity among the people brought together by centuries of empire-building endeavors (Elving, 2020).

Predominantly, the swift pronouncement of the EPRDF to expel citizens according to their racial profiles has caused exogenous political shockwaves and upshots across the nation (Goitom, 2019). Ethnic intolerance grew and gained momentum, and ethnic violence became a permanent fixture of Ethiopian politics (Dewey, 2017). Certain ethnic groups have been persistent, victimized, evicted, and displaced from the places they have been living since birth just for who they are. In this regard, hundreds of innocent Ethiopians have been forcefully evacuated by unidentified assailants (Abdu, 2019).

During the withdrawal so many have been murdered in the outbreak, some trying to defend themselves and their loved ones, while others demanding others to relinquish and evacuate (Gedamu, 2018). In short, when ethnic interests and ethnic politics become the modus operandi, the challenges emanating from it rapidly become overwhelming to the government to handle and manage them (Aden, 2018) and (Turton, 2016).

The government was pushed by certain political circumstances and instabilities of the country to the point where it was compelled to embark on implementing forceful actions to undermine the pressure (Dahir, Ethiopia's previously divided ethnic groups are unifying to protest against the government, 2016). The security forces, backed by the standing rule at various levels, have habitually used live ammunition to disband and diffuse these protests, killing hundreds, and arresting tens of thousands (Woods, 2020).

State security forces have consistently used excessive and lethal force against largely peaceful protests that have swept through the Oromia and Amhara regional states (Tekle, 2019). Despite the tragic catastrophe, the protests, which were motivated by a series of public grievances, ultimately led to the outrageous and despicable resignation of Prime Minster Hailemariam Desalegn in 2018 (Moore, 2018).

Immediately after the acknowledgment of the letter of resignation, the lately appointed Prime Minister Abiy Ahmed lifted the state of emergency, ordered the release of thousands of prisoners, allowed exiled dissidents to return home, and unblocked hundreds of websites and TV channels. Since then, the protests appeared to ominously slow down (Giorgis, 2018). Nevertheless, these actions significantly slackened the protests, the ethnic-based clashes relentlessly got sustained.

The incompetence and failure of the new office to implement the rule of law, the exacerbation of ethnic-based jingoism, and the splintering of the EPRDF aggravated the state of the internal affairs of the country to the worst (Badwaza, 2019). Egypt and Sudan have also pushed a lot of external pressure on the governments to prevent the completion of the Great Dam, under construction in Ethiopia[17].

Social media, such as Facebook, Twitter, Instagram, and YouTube, and the Internet, in general, have been expansively used in inciting, agitating, and rousing citizens to contest the system (Feigenbaum, 2018). These media, in a way, have become an outlet for an enormous animosity and acrimony bubbled up in the country as a result of the racial politics which has been instigated for the last three conservative years (Jeffrey, Ethnic Violence in Ethiopia Stoked by Social Media from U.S., 2018).

The platforms of these social media have facilitated the organization of protests around racism across the nation and as a result of which many have been persecuted, tortured, and killed. For instance, after the killing of Hachalu Hundessa has been circulated over social media extensively, substantial violence has been reported with multiple people killed in ongoing protests (Ghedamu, 2020).

The Ethiopian diaspora groups, most importantly, the political activities kept calling for global protests both around the world and within the nation. Therefore, a lot of fatal and tragic protests kept occurring in multiple cities at the same time. (Endeshaw, 2020). This became a solemn headache to the presiding party.

Though there is a great irony in government castigating social platforms and threatening to regulate them, while simultaneously being utterly dependent on those very platforms to secure their reelections and listen to their citizenry, the Ethiopian government unreservedly singled out social media as a fostering factory of the violence in driving the unrest now absorbing the entire country (Schemm, 2016).

---

[17] Solomon Gizaw (January 10, 2020), Identity Politics and Its Impact on Public Passion for Digital Marketing, Interview by Daniel Solomon

The practice of determinedly banning any type of protest, shouting down the Internet, and blocking social media got to be a routine phenomenon (Samuel, 2020), upsetting the public passion for digital marketing and any other online activities (Mumo, 2019). For instance, on the 22nd date of June 2019, Ethiopia had rushed into an internet blackout following what the government described as a failed attempted coup in the Amhara region (Muthoki, 2019). Likewise, on June 30, 2020, CJP has stated a nationwide Internet shutdown in Ethiopia (CJP, 2020).

Though the real objective of many state-sanctioned internet blackouts is to keep protests in check, the outages mean a lot to the Internet users and even more so to the economic growth of the country. It has always a kind of instant and intense damage. During these outages, digital marketing had been made unnavigable. Businesses could not participate in e-commerce. They could not deliver digital products and services. In short, people could not interconnect using online menses.

The growth effect of these outages is colossal. For instance, in 2011, Egypt was worried about its street protest and blocked the Internet for about 5 consecutive days. In the aftermath of the shutdown, the Organization for Economic Development and Cooperation (OECD) found that the decision to cut connectivity all over the country just for five days cost Egypt $90 million (Mickoleit, 2011).

In the same vein, the Ethiopian government cut off the internet across most of the country after the fatal shooting of musician and activist Hachalu Hundessa. The blackout took place on 30 June 2020 and went on for 23 straight days, interfering with Ethiopians' rights to access information and muzzling any vestige of freedom of expression. This outage has cost the country a total of $102 million (El-Sherbiny, 2021).

These few but expository examples of Internet outages in Ethiopia and elsewhere in Africa could tell a lot about the position of the respective regimes on the Internet. They seem to shout it down whenever they have a fear of public unrest for some reason. This violates the right of the citizens to Internet access, also known as the right to broadband or freedom to connect.

According to this right, citizens have the right to access the Internet to exercise themselves in any way they want. The states have a responsibility to ensure that Internet access is broadly available. It also restricts them not to unreasonably restrict an individual's access to the Internet.

On top of these violations by the state, according to some sources, the régimes do not seem to invest in the expansion of the Internet adequately for various reasons. First, they have some other pressing needs seeing for their immediate attention, such as war, drought, instability, and lies. Second, they don't have the budget to invest in the area. Last, they may lack the interest to invest in the area for fear it can cause a lot more social instability than there is on the ground (Latif, 2017).

More interestingly, they do not have the gut to permit the private sector to put their hands in the field. For instance, the State-owned monopoly Ethio -Telecom is the only Internet provider in Ethiopia to date (Burkitt-Gray, 2018). On the contrary, as long as there is no political stability in their respective countries, they would persistently continue to suppress the sector (Ambaye, 2019), (Ademo, 2012), and (Abdu, 2019).

Most of these shouts down incident has nation-scale impact affecting cellular and fixed-line networks and are not attributed to any international issue, technical outage, or cyber-attack (Internet cut in Ethiopia, 2020).

On the contrary, some researchers indicate that over the past two decades, with the rapid development and popularization of world internet and computer technology, the internet has been an integral part of both human daily life and the financial market (Rapid development and popularization of the Internet, 2021).

This growth has significantly impacted the global economy has been transformed by digitization and rapid technological changes, boosting e-commerce, engaging new actors, and presenting novel possibilities (Rapid Development of Information Technology in the 20th Century, 2019).

In support of this perception (Blanke, 2016) argues the unprecedented speed of change, as well as the breadth and the depth of many radical changes unleashed by new digital, robotic, and 3D technologies, is having major impacts on what we produce and do, how and where we do it and indeed how we earn a living.

The contexts of global trade can be connected towards shaping the nature and the outcomes of digitization, including towards realizing sustainable development outcomes (Lajevardi, 2016). It can also play a significant role in the effort towards promoting essential development efforts and poverty reduction.

Besides, the communication effort in digital marketing is becoming precise, personal, interesting, interactive, and social and, therefore, it has come to be a good platform for socialization, friend rising, and getting to know each other (T Stephen, 2016). Creating due awareness and attentiveness which include both recall and recognition has become the first step for any further move towards a successful market strategy.

In the end, the statement of the problem emanates from this act of continuous outage, and less availability and affordability of the Internet in Ethiopia. The outage is underscored as a deliberate act of the government to manage the social upheavals caused by the racial identity politics currently underway in the country.

This practice does not only hold back the public passion for digital marketing, but it is also paving the way for the digital divide down the road. Hence, on top of persistent institutional, regulatory, knowledge, and skills irregularities, as well as limitations on physical infrastructure that affect connectivity, their practice of identity politics in Ethiopia is becoming a probable concern for the fast reduction of public passion and the occurrence of a digital divide in the country.

1.4. Purpose of the Study

Since 1991 Ethiopia has implemented a federal system that targets accommodating diversity. However, to date, federalism has only been superficially used and practiced in Ethiopia. Since the constitution was established in 1995, the then EPRDF, which has recently rehabilitated into PP, has maintained power through monocratic means (Gebreluel, 2019).

As this federalism was distinctively established based on a racial the ethnic identity of citizens, it doomed to create more problems than the solutions it was sought to bring about. These problems are too many and too diverse to deal with in one single academic research. They must be seen in a better depth and width from different perspectives, filed of studies, degrees of concern, and intestines.

The purpose of the research is to methodically examine the impact of identity politics on the public passion for digital marketing and suggest proper recommendations to all concerned parties. It also attempts to suggest a country-level risk management framework that would help reverse the adverse situation in the country. Besides, the study finds out if identity political could endanger the country to the digital divide.

1.5. Research Questions

There are three basic questions that this research would like to address:

1. Is there any significant relationship between identity politics and public passion for digital marketing?
2. Can identity politics lead to a digital divide when public passion for digital marketing diminishes?
3. Can identity politics establish a country-level political risk in developing countries such as Ethiopia?
4. What kind of risk management framework would best help such countries to reverse the course of the problem?

1.6. Assumptions and Hypothesis

Since the introduction of identity politics in Ethiopia by EPRDF at the beginning of the 1990s, the country has never been a calm and cool nation for its citizens (Gizaw, 2020). Its people could not make it together for the lack of love and dignity to each other. Hatred has become rampant. The abhorrence that has been injected into the system, along with the ethnic-based political structure established in the name of federalism, and the political heaviness exploring here and there has turned Ethiopia to be a sort of unstable country (Asfaw, 2015).

The action of taking the key rights to land, government jobs, representation to local and federal bodies, away from the individual citizens, and giving them to the so-called nations and nationalities by the government was the root cause for the political upheavals emerging across the country (Mahmood,

2019). Individuals lost their rights for the nationality they belong to. People born from multiple nationalities, for instance, from Amhara Father and Oromo mother, have no place in the system. For instance, most of the inhabitants of Addis Ababa, the capital of Africa, do not ascribe themselves to a certain ethnic background[18].

Particularly the very narrative of Ethiopia's current federalism which implicit a kind of an explicit assumption that the main motivating factor behind the struggle against the military regime, Derg was Amhara oppression has been dangerous. It has convinced quite a great number of people to consider Amhara as an oppressor and tyrant.

Hence, they were motivated and triggered to fight the people of Amhara to get rid of them in one or another way. The Tigrayan Peoples Liberation Front (TPLF), for instance, believed that the root cause of oppression and injustice in Ethiopia lies in "Amhara's chauvinistic great nation" mentality, thus making its struggle a *de facto* attempt to eliminate this mentality within the Amhara (Tesfaye, 2018).

Such a narrative has caused continuous political turmoil instigating instability, unsteadiness, and volatility all over the country. In response to the public reaction, internet blackouts are increasingly becoming popular especially for political reasons (Ambaye, 2019). What is more, concerned authorities do not seem to invest any better to expand digitalization in the country. This, in turn, has given a clue of the prevalence of the danger of the digital divide.

Therefore, this research assumes that identity politics can result in political repression, dictatorial internet monopoly by government, unfortunate economy, poor level of education, and

---

[18] Solomon Gizaw (January 10, 2020), Identity Politics and Its Impact on Public Passion for Digital Marketing, Interview by Daniel Solomon

wicked currency, all these corporate dynamics affecting the progress of digitalization and by so doing digital marketing. If counteractive actions are not taken in due time and the political instability continues to get worsens, the country might suffer from the digital divide.

The incidence of the digital divide is probable. In other words, the research hypothesizes that there is a significant relationship between identity-based politics and public passion for digital marketing, which might lead to the digital divide. On the contrary, the null hypothesis is that there is no significant relationship between identity-based politics and the said public passion, which in turn confirms the non-occurrence of a digital divide in any way.

The hypothesis is, therefore, there is a significant relationship between public passion for digital marketing and identity-driven politics, which also denotes the probability for the prevalence of the digital divide as aftermath. Likewise, the null hypothesis assumes the non-existence of any relationship between the variables, public passion, and identity-based politics, which in turn circumvents the prevalence of the digital divide.

The finding of the research indicates that there is a significant relation between identity-driven politics and public passion for digital marketing. The predominance of the former expressively affects the presence of the latter, casing over 7% probability for the manifestation of the digital divide.

1.7. Significance of the Study

The ever-growing consumption of the Internet is being perceived as the most important factor to reinforce the social and economic development of any given society at any corner of the world (Selwyn, 2001). Therefore, any academic research that has to do with anything associated with the Internet has quite a several significance. To mention some but few, the first Internet has become the critical vehicle for young adults to maintain their social presence and extend social connections (ShihuiFeng, 2019).

Second, the Internet offers a possibly innovative medium for academic research, dissemination of news, opinions, promotions, reports, discourse about practical, theoretical, and spiritual issues (Hannah, 1998). Third, participation on the Internet for playing games and enjoying entertainment, making friends, raising funds, doing promotions, performing digital marketing and any other online business is growing rapidly (Menu, 2008). Fourth, the Internet plays a significant role in the routine lives of virtually over 40% of the world's population, and it is becoming increasingly entwined in everyday life situations (Samuel D, 2014).

The Internet permits the formation of new public spheres easily without the constraints of geography, time, and political interest. It allows users to connect and restructure society by renegotiating rules. What is more, the Internet supports the way innovation is being carried out enabling societies to live sustainably. In short, the Internet touches upon every single piece and plot of life which makes it a boiling topic in the contemporary world (Araba Sey, 2013), (Edewor, 2011), and (Oak, 2018).

The Internet has made it simple to meet with quite a several people across the board easily and commendably. If we take the USA in 2009, we had 74% of its adult population (18 years old and above) spending quite a considerable amount of time on the Internet (Lee, 2010). Likewise, the rate of Internet use in China among the surveyed adolescents for specific research was 88% (Cao, 2014) of which 2.4% have shown a sign of Internet addiction.

Hence, as many tend to spend time on the Internet, researching matters that matter for the mainstream gives the research a point of significance, whatsoever. All said, digital technologies have and will continue to have a significant impact (P.K.Kannan, 2017).

In recent days, the demand for digital marketing, which is the promotion of products or brands online, has become increasingly high (Parvez, 2016). Different research conducted in the last decade, indicate that one of the most significant changes in the business environment has been the implementation of digital marketing strategies to capitalize on the ROI with less LOE (Saura J. R., 2018) and (Saura J. R., 2017).

The internal structure and strategies of some companies have transformed advancing towards a digital environment influenced by various Internet business models and digital marketing strategies (Pandey, 2020). In other words, the rapidly emerging digital economy is challenging the relevance of existing marketing practices (Wymbs, 2011).

Despite the fast-growing popularity of electronic commerce and the presence of many companies on the virtual market, the opportunities offered by this new environment are still unknown (Kiani, 2020). Some of the researches that are available in the area focus on subject matters that include but are not limited to the successful cases of digital marketing (Liu, 2019), the new threats of digital marketing (Kathryn, 2012).

Other studies emphasized various marketing strategies that are commonly used in digital media (Katherine, 2010), the use of web analytics for digital marketing performance measurement (lJoelJärvinen, 2015).

Still were some other researchers who paid due attention to definite and selected subject matters as the digital marketing skills gap and developing a digital marketer model for the communication industries (Royle, 2014), fraud, and other scam related issues associated with digital marketing (Kaur, 2016), and some current and future trends in digital marketing (Bala, 2020).

Be that as it may, as indicated above this research is not enough to cover all the pressing issues in the field. Hence, this research is significant in that it adds meaningful scientific research in the digital marketing field of study and by so doing contributes to the skills and services achieved thus far. The result of the study can be used for future research in this field.

Digital marketing without adequate access to computers and the Internet is a futile exercise. Hence, the question of accessibility and affordability of the Internet has become an increasingly important factor in the growth of digital marketing around the world. It goes without saying that to completely immerse oneself in the economic, political, and social aspects of life. Nonetheless, the degree to which people have access to the Internet is causing major apartheid and segregation across the world (Kaveh, 2016).

Analysis of the Internet use among countries depicts enormous variation displaying the pivotal role of the Internet in everyday life (Rrostcki, 2020). Most of the researches that have been conducted on factors that could lead to the birth of the digital divide, differences in income and literacy are identified as the most significant contributors (Warshauer, 2019), (Cisler, 2001) and (Schmutzer, 2001).

Apart from explaining the effect of the racial insights on access to the Internet, at least to the current knowledge of the researcher, there is no adequate scientific study that explains how xenophobic exclusionary tribal political ideology affect the public passion to digital marketing paving the way to the threat of digital divide.

The paucity of systematic studies in the area by itself would mark the significance of the research great. Also, as an eye-opener, it might trigger others to do more comprehensive research in the area. Moreover, by sending a signal about the danger of running such a top-down imposed exclusionary political tribal ideology to the future of Ethiopia, the research would be of great importance locally to the political party currently in the office and all other active parties in the country.

The popularity of the Internet around the world has created quite enormous discussions and debates (WPT, 2012), (Pathmalal, 2013), and (Wiener, 2018). Some scholars such as (Surbhi, 2018), (Carr, 2011), and (Hussain, 2012) emphasize the information gaps that might be created between developed and developing countries.

According to them, the world populations may soon be divided into groups of inequality as 'information elite' and 'information ignorant'. On the other hand, some scholars are concerned about some of the vigorous roots and origins of such a gap which usually is known as the digital divide (Fong, 2017), (Arthur, 2017), and (Kuyoro Shade O, 2012).

However, in both cases, the swift growths in technology have stressed the greater complexities associated with this scientific incongruence. This signifies how important the topic is all around the world. It looks as if it is a cross-cutting global issue affecting all of us as one single community living in this small village called the world.

Therefore, scientific research, such as this, on such topics should be encouraged and stimulated. The outcome of such research would have much more significance for quite a lot of people affianced in the digital business arena and the policymakers of their respective countries.

The digital divide can penetrate locally deep down within a given country as well and by so doing surface the gap out gaudily on the podium (Laura, 2015). In other words, according to some scholars, the technological disparity can also happen within a single country, rather than between developed and developing countries (Review, 2019). (Negririo, 2015), (Hibert, 2016), and (Wharton, 2019). This marks another implication on the prominence of the theme of this study.

The substance seems to be crucially imperative to every single country that would like to work well away from the danger of the digital divide. Therefore, countries that are on the verge of their disintegration due to their respective political upheavals might take this study as a life support mechanic to continue to live so that they might get little more time to reverse situations that county negative to their growth.

ICTs can be a powerful tool for increasing transparency and facilitating information and communication processes among stakeholders (Hasani, 2015), and by so doing it might help to minimize some of the critical leadership enigmas. The digital world may lead to increased democratization (Cervellati, 2011) by enabling citizens or constituents to participate in the decision-making process of policymakers and government through the electronic channel (Belcastro, 2010).

However, to fetch water at this level, e-democracy has yet to reach its ideal level of actualization in the political participation process (Fong, 2017). The past few decades have witnessed a widening of the digital divide among countries in the world (San M.-c. L., 2018), (Elisa, 2008) and (David, 2009).

Connecting the dots, in this contemporary world digital divide has now become an important development concern of many governments (Taylor, 2018) and (James, 2003). Most of the research works conducted before this one, look at the

Internet's popularity and the positive impact it has imposed on the world economy by large, which makes this research inimitably important as a triggering socket for other research to plunge into the area and work on such topics on countries like Ethiopia whose identity-based exclusive politics is wounding its actuality.

The outcome of this research is quintessential to a country like Ethiopia which is still struggling with ethnic-based political creed casing quite several paradoxes both on the politics and economy of the country. If these problems are not well analyzed and concerned parties take counteractive action in due time, it would cost the country more than it could pay to reverse the situation.

The result of the study could help policymakers make informed decisions about expanding the Internet service across the country and by so doing facilitate digital marketing. What is more, it could also save the nation from deteriorating into a digital divide.

1.8. Scope of the Study

Marketing, be it digital or otherwise, is a set of activities related to creating, communicating, delivering, and exchanging offerings that have value for others (Kiani, 2020) and (Kiani, 2020). It is the act of connecting with customers with a bid to convince them towards buying a product or subscribing to a service (Jiwa, Marketing: A Love Story: How to Matter to Your Customers, 2016).

It is one of the key activities that every business must partake in, as no business can survive without effective marketing and publicity (Diamond, 2018). In other words, in any business, the function of marketing is to bring value to customers, whom the business seeks to identify, satisfy, and retain (Varghese, 2017) and (Kingsnorth, Digital Marketing Strategy: An Integrated Approach to Online Marketing, 2019).

Digital marketing is any action carried out using any electronic media towards the promotion of goods and services. This is a primarily Internet-based activity aimed at selling goods or providing services. In 2015, the International Telecommunication Union estimated about 3.2 billion people, or almost half of the world's population, would be online by the end of the year (Internet used by 3.2 billion people in 2015, 2015).

The number of people using the Internet has surged over the past few years, with more than one million people coming online for the first time each day since January 2018. There are 4.39 billion internet users in 2019, an increase of 366 million (9 percent) versus January 2018. (KEMP, 2019). After this prompt development of ICT, over the past two decades, the global economy has been transformed by quick digitization and apt technical transformation, boosting e-commerce, engaging new actors, and presenting novel possibilities (Cavallo, 2016). This has generated quite a significant input towards the massive influence of the industry over the overall economy of the world (Chan, 2016).

Estimates published by e-Marketer, a news and research site on digital trends, put global e-commerce website sales at above US$22 trillion last year, with projections that they will expand to US$27 trillion by 2020 (WTO, 2017). This displays how big the range and coverage of the digital market in the economy of the contemporary world is.

In this enormous economy, there can be a tone wide-ranging topic that could be realistic to discourse them in academic research such as this. Nevertheless, for various reasons the researcher has limited the scope of this study to the threat of identity-based exclusive politics which is currently fettering the expansion of digital marketing in developing countries with a special focus on Facebook marketing.

On the other hand, the past few decades have witnessed a widening of the digital divide among countries in the world. Connecting this global digital divide to the dearth of access by the public to the internet in certain developing countries has now become an important development policy of many governments in the developing world (San M.-c. L., 2006).

The possible cause to this deficiency could be anything from poverty to poor education, from lack of peace to political instability, from the dearth of internet availability to misuse of the internet, or any other, this study has given due attention only to identity-based exclusive politics practiced by developing nations. It does not go deep into all other possible roots and grounds, for fear the research might go overwhelming in terms of coverage and size.

The number of developing countries suffering from bad internet accessibility is well over 130 (ISI, 2018). Currently, where technology has modernized every aspect of human existence, it is hard to imagine that there are countries that seem to have never felt the effects of modernity and the benefits of human advancements (Chang, 2019). Others are plagued with economic turmoil, political unrest, and civil wars, making it hard for their nations to go and rise above and beyond the pangs of the poverty line.

Togo is the first in the row with a GDP per capita of $899 while Madagascar and Afghanistan with GDP per capita of $934 and $956.00, respectively (Chang, 2019). However, this research does not cover all these countries even if they have the fear of getting into the digital divide any time soon, given their respective political, social, and economic circumstance. Instead, the research focused on Ethiopia mainly because Ethiopia is the only country that the research was able to get adequate quantity and quality of data. Attempts have been made to engage some more countries, but the data issue was almost unbearable.

It is vivid that the digital divide has both policy and managerial implications (Dewan, 2018), and understanding these implications is a worthwhile area of research. On the policy side, the key question is what should be done to close the gap between the haves and have-nots in local communities and the global arena. Some studies such as (Gallardo, 2018), (Devaraj, 2017), (Mandel, 2017) and (Perrin, 2015) have focused on the policy implication of the digital divide while some others like (Sun, 2011) and (Kuo, 2011) emphasized only the managerial side of it. The scope of this study, on the contrary, has made an appropriate attempt to comprise both sides of the story.

Taxes, tariffs, trade, and legislation, and funding for public access points are examples of research themes that could be studied to find out the influence of access to the Internet and the Internet, and thereby figure out the progress of the divide. There could be much more interesting, appealing, and very significant research areas on the digital divide. However, the attention of this research has always been only on the divide that could be caused by political injustice, monopoly of the Internet by the government, and political decisions beyond and above the power of law.

1.9. Limitation of the Study

One of the major limitations of research on digital marketing originates from the instantaneous alterations that engross the various artifacts that the industry is grounded on. For instance, some of the mainstream research conducted on digital marketing tend to focus on matters that link the consumer, customer, and the marketer through information used to identify and define marketing opportunities and problems (Akrani, 2013). Still, are others emphasizing assessing marketing actions, monitor performance, and understanding marketing as a process (Bala, 2020).

Since as all these factors keep on a consistent change, the research result may not be able to give a kind of recommendation that would significantly help to eradicate the problem from its root (Reda, 2018). Even if it does, the problem is subject to consistent changes, thus, the findings of the research may not far be reaching. Thus, to lessen the impact emanating from the immensity of digital marketing, the study is determined only to find out the impact of triable politics on the public passion for digital marketing.

Digital marketing is an immense economy, wide-ranging in quite a few areas. This market creates a bundle of goods and services that the company offers at a price to its customers. The bundle consists of a tangible good, an intangible service or benefit, and the price of the offering. This is a product from a given company reaching out to customers through the Internet.

This, by itself, is a massive range of study points that is impossible to cover in research like this. Nevertheless, when we add up all other products available on the shelve coming from various companies, it would even be more problematic to manage. To do away with this issue, the study has limited itself to the passion of customers who would wish to do digital marketing without considering the product they want to deal with.

The other limitation of this study comes from the very nature of the digital divide which is a universal topic and a new feature of existing variation among digital users. Several researchers have used the term digital divide to differentiate between people who can gain control over technologies and master digital skills than others.

It has most commonly been used to illustrate the view that certain individuals are not able to obtain access to personal computers or the Internet due to a variety of factors including race, socio-economic status, age, gender, place of residence, level of education, adeptness with technology, and/or social associations (Srihari, 2016), (Norries, 2009) and (Chinn, 2004). Upholding this description, (Snyder, 2013) says the gap between those with and those without access to computers and the Internet and, as a result, their participation in the information age.

The extensive exposure of the explanation of the digital divide by itself exhibits how wide-ranging the topic would be even while seen from the possible delineations given to the digital divide alone. One of the limitations of this research work emanates from this perspective. For convenience's sake, it does not endeavor to cover all the potential descriptions that have been forwarded to define the digital divide. Instead, it sees the matter only from the point of veracities of how it recounts in the study area.

Secondly, factors affecting the digital divide are too many (John, 2019). Some of them may be beyond the control of the individual (Kaigo, 2002), others are related to personal choices (Warschauer, 2004), such as when one has an aversion to technology and so chooses, for one reason or another, people might decide not to make use of such technologies.

According to (Ademo, 2012) and (Sharziz, 2014), as the Internet grew in popularity during the mid-1990s, the digital divide took on political and public policy overtones as certain groups and policymakers claimed that some individuals were being left behind in the digital revolution and would have trouble catching up.

These leftovers are scattered all over the world. Plus, the reasons that have put the same behind varies across the board. Therefore, it would be very much riotous and unmanageable even to consider every single one of them into the attention of this research paper. That would explode the research and hinder it from fetching its objective. Therefore, this research has deliberately omitted all apart from Ethiopia.

Thirdly, understanding the divide, in a nutshell, is imperative but not that easy (Understanding the Digital Divide, 2010). The digital divide has a profound impact on how firms compete globally, how they relate to their customers and business partners, and how they formulate their strategies for online commerce.

In other words, it is all a complex staff involved in it. Nevertheless, it would become unamenable to even attempt to cover all the details in the arena. For the sake of manageability this research limit itself to a digital divide that could be created due to political causes.

In conclusion, the research heavenly depends on data collected from primary resources, mainly users. This is so because there is no significant research that has been conducted as yet on the digital divide or any other related subject matter with a focus on Ethiopia and the identity politics that governs the current system in the country.

Chapter Two

REVIEW OF RELATED LITERATURE

A REVIEW OF PERTINENT LITERATURE is the process of collecting, selecting, and reviewing books, journals, reports, abstracts, and other reference materials (McCombes, 2019). It provides an overview of current knowledge, allowing you to identify relevant theories, methods, and gaps in the existing research. In this regard, this chapter presents the literature that has been scanned, reviewed, studied, and analyzed in the research. The chapter has ten strategic parts. The first part gives reasonable background on the historical signposts on the history and political culture of Ethiopia. The second part discusses identity politics in current Ethiopia.

The second part emphases the influence of identity politics in Ethiopia. It attempts to answer the following questions. What is identity politics? How did identity politics get into Ethiopia? Who introduced it? What danger is it causing in the country? It also touches upon other facts that qualify identity politics as a major country-level risk on the political environment of the country.

The third part is about the advancement of technology and digital marketing. It investigates the subject from a worldwide perspective. However, the review does not include the pros and cons of the various stages its advancement has been through. Instead, it emphasizes some of the key milestones to its expansion and development across the world.

The fourth one concentrates on the availability and accessibility of the Internet in Ethiopia. In a way, it deliberates on Internet penetration, number of users, affordability of the

Internet, and other relevant issues. It also pinpoints identity politics as the major impairment on the effort of the government to advance the progress of the Internet in the country.

The fifth and the sixth pars discuss the impact of the Internet on the political affairs of the world and Ethiopia, respectively. The chapter brings forth how the Internet has become very influential in the current political milieu of the world. It also confers its effect on the day-to-day ongoing of the current Ethiopian politics.

Likewise, the seventh chapter deals with the impact of the Internet on the Ethiopian economy. It highlights the economic damage incurred by the country as the result of the continued shutdowns of the Internet practiced by the government of Ethiopia to suppress the political upheavals. It also highlights some of the violations of basic rights of the citizens of Ethiopia at a time when they need to stay informed about the routines of the political activities in the country.

Then there is another part that talks about the probability of the incidence of the digital divide in Ethiopia as an aftermath of identity politics. This part answers two basic questions: What the digital divide is? What does it impact if it occurs?

In the end, there is a theoretical framework designed to help properly direct the research. This is important to understand the trends and themes that have been going thru the political culture of the nation that led to contemporary Ethiopia. The framework suggests a risk management tool that would support the stakeholders to handle some of the perplexity and impact of identity politics in the country.

2.1. Historical Millstones in Ethiopian Politics

Ethiopia is strategically located in east-central Africa, bordered on the west by Sudan, the east by Somalia and Djibouti, the south by Kenya, and the northeast by Eritrea. It has several high mountains, the highest of which is Ras Dashan at 15,158 ft (4,620 m) (Infoplease, 2019), (Chigozie, 2019), and (Bada, 2017). The Blue Nile, or Abbai, rises in the northwest and flows in a great semicircle before entering Sudan (Afrito, 2019). The second largest lake in Africa, Lake Tana, lies in the northwest (Ethiopia, 2019).

People have lived in Ethiopia for thousands of years (Kaplan, 2015) and (Tim, 2019). However, the first well-known kingdom in Ethiopia rose in the first century AD (The kingdom of Aksum: from the 5th century BC, 2019). Some historians such as (Foerster, 2019), (Sullivan, 2019), and (Tim, 2019) believe the fact that by 100 AD a kingdom called Axum existed in Ethiopia. According to (Lambert, 2019) Axum had a sort of trade enactment with such countries as Rome, Arabia, and India.

Modern Ethiopia, which has been materialized under the rule of Sovereign Menelik II, who established its independence by routing an Italian invasion in 1896 (Raugh, 2014), was much known for its independence, unity, and sovereignty of its citizens, rule of law, and dignity of man. When Menelik II died, his grandson, Lij Iyassu, succeeded to the throne but soon lost support because of his Muslim ties. He was deposed in 1916 by the Christian nobility, and Menelik's daughter, Zauditu, was made empress. Her cousin, Ras Tafari Makonnen, was made regent and successor to the throne (Marcus, 1995).

Emperor Haile Selassie banned slavery and tried to consolidate his dispersed realm, in which well over 70 languages were spoken (Zewde, 2001). In 1931, he produced a constitution, revised in 1955, that called for a parliament with an allotted senate, an elected chamber of deputies, and a system of courts. Nonetheless, basic power remained with the emperor (Ethiopia profile - Timeline, 2019).

Later, after a period of civil unrest that began in February 1974, a provisional administrative council of soldiers, known as the Derg ("committee"), seized power from the aging Emperor Haile Selassie I on September 12, 1974, and installed a government that was socialist in name and military in style (Meredith, 2005).

Eventually, a political group called the EPRDF came to power by an armed struggle against the military government in 1991, and in May a separatist guerrilla organization, the Eritrean People's Liberation Front, took control of the province of Eritrea (de Waal, 1997). The two groups agreed that Eritrea would have an internationally supervised referendum on independence, without the consent of citizens.

This election took place in April 1993 with almost unanimous support for Eritrean independence (Chanie, 2007). Then, the Ethiopian Peoples' Revolutionary Democratic Front (EPRDF), led by its chairman and prime minister, Meles Zenawi, has radically reformed Ethiopia's political system.

The regime transformed the hitherto centralized state into the Federal Democratic Republic and redefined citizenship, politics, and identity on ethnic grounds (ICG, 2019). They introduced a sort of identity-based exclusive politics that has incurred the country a tremendous number of lives and resources.

To date, federalism has only been nominally practiced in Ethiopia. Since the constitution was established in 1995, the ruling Ethiopian People's Revolutionary Democratic Front (EPRDF) has maintained power through autocratic means.

Ethiopians in the nine regional states have never had the privilege of electing their governors. These officials have instead most of the time been appointed through informal channels by the EPRDF leadership in Addis Ababa. However, very lately the formation of the new Ethiopian Prosperity Party (PP) has substituted the EPRDF.

Disbanding the ruling EPRDF and forming a new national party, or what some refer to as a Pan-Ethiopian party, is daring. Though the move from EPRDF to PP has been accomplished with a lot of cost of troubles and encounters, the notion of self-rule, which is the fundamental principle of ethnonational federalism, has never been practiced to date in its fullest sense. This, in turn, has resulted in political instability that has caused thousands of innocent lives across the nation.

All said, the geopolitical location of the country along with its history of shielding its freedom as a sovereign country against the then colonizer Italy and it's being the origin of the Blue Nile upon which Egypt and Sudan depend for their water consumption has made Ethiopia politically the center of attention worldwide. Its frequent attempt to grow and get rid of poverty have been significantly impacted and undermined by external factors.

In this regard, the construction of the great Dam in the country is worth mentioning. Being an 85% contributor to the water of the Blue Nile, Ethiopia has a lot of pressures from all over to build the Dam. On top of that, the identity politics which has been recently introduced to the country has complicated the enigma far more,

2.2. Identify Politics in Current Ethiopia

According to Webster's dictionary, identity politics is a state of condition in which groups of people having a particular racial, religious, ethnic, social, or cultural identity tend to promote their specific interests or concerns without regard to the interests or concerns of any larger political group[19]. Identity politics is the act of targeting groups for political gain based on some common demographic (Brown, 2020). The fundamental problem with identity politics is that it is the politics of division (Keith, 2019).

Identity politics took its modern shape and form during the second half of the last century, following the footprints of modernism (Thomas, 2019). It emerged as an emancipatory mode of political action and thinking based on the shared experience of injustice by groups, notably blacks, women, gays, Latinos, and American Indians (Martin, 2019). It is often presented as the politics of inclusion but, is about giving preferential treatment through laws, taxes, or social norms to a group (Shillington, 2017).

Identity politics has become prevalent worldwide since modernism (Gonzalez, 2019). It came to office in Ethiopia at the end of the Cold War, after the socialist military regime in Ethiopia was overthrown by the nationalist armed forces, EPRDF. This force which came to power in 1991 has adopted a federal system, which is explicitly based on ethnicity, to radically reconstruct the Ethiopian state as a multi-ethnic federation[20].

Since then, many Sub-Saharan African countries find themselves overwhelmed by chronic ethnic tensions that often corrupt into violent conflicts (Mengisteab, 2018). Such ethnic tensions have not only depleted the finical resources of the continent but also, they have contributed to the region's growing marginalization from the global economic system.

---

[19] Dictionary by Merriam-Webster (2020), America's most trusted online dictionary for English word definitions, meanings, and pronunciation.
[20] Hargewoyin Meresha (January 12, 2020), Identity Politics and Its Impact on Public Passion for Digital Marketing, Interview by Daniel Solomon

Discussing the common factors contributing to this drawback, (Mengisteab, 2018) thinks bad corruptions, paucity of self-governance, and self-serving dictators, which have strongly linked with identity-based exclusive politics are worth mentioning. For much of the last year, the ethnic strain has exploded to the most awful level In (Mengisteab, 2018).

To mention some but few, Ethiopians, especially in the vast Oromo community, have been protesting the government over corruption, lack of jobs, and poor administration. Their efforts have been championed by many Ethiopian dissidents living abroad, especially in the United States, who have held rallies for them and bombarded social media sites with denunciations of the regime's harsh suppression of protests (Paul, 2014).

Ethnic conflicts are not new, but the levels of violence being witnessed today are very disturbing (How ethnic violence is destabilizing Ethiopia's reform gains, 2018). This was so because, the coalition, known as the EPRDF, which is the author of contemporary Ethiopian politics, was made up of four ethnic parties:

The Oromo Peoples' Democratic Organization, Amhara National Democratic Movement, Southern Ethiopian People's Democratic Movement, and the TPLF. After the coalition came together, it introduced an ethnic federal system of governance to attempt and address historic ethnic grievances by giving citizens the chance to administer themselves (Abdu, 2019).

This federal system, in turn, allowed regions to organize along tribal lines. It also led to the rise of the nationalist movements, which eventually weakened Ethiopia's national unity[21]. Since then, ethnic intolerance grew and gained

---

[21] Solomon Gizaw (January 12, 2020), Identity Politics and Its Impact on Public Passion for Digital Marketing, Interview by Daniel Solomon

momentum, and ethnic violence became a permanent fixture of Ethiopian politics (Bedasso, 2018).

Given the four constitutive parties of the front are organized along ethnic lines, the distribution of economic and political resources has also taken place through ethnic-based patronage structures[22]. This includes both the legal distribution of official posts in the government, as well as the illicit benefits accrued through some of these positions.

The distribution of power and resources from seats in the cabinet to leadership positions in universities are often based on an informal ethnic quota system (Bedasso, 2018) adds. With more than 80 nationalities and ethnic groups, Ethiopia's political landscape is dominated by tribal allegiances (Ethiopia's ethnic conflicts destabilize Abiy's reforms, 2019).

These fidelities have never been able to quench the political dryness of society. On the contrary, identity-based politics cracked the danger of disintegrating the country. In many parts of the country, the new political atmosphere has permitted long-running strains between communities to erupt into conflict as hate speech has flourished. In total, 2.9 million people had been displaced by December 2018, more than those dislodged in Syria, Yemen, Somalia, and Afghanistan combined, according to estimates published this month (Wilsson, 2019).

Ethnic militias are committing vigilante violence, killing local government officials, burning homes, and raping women, according to Addis-based officials, diplomats, and aid workers (Fick, 2019). Ethnic massacres have also been reported on university campuses in Tigray and Amhara as students turned on students, due to their ethnic profile.

Some report indicates public universities have seen

---

[22] Cyrus Hailu (January 12, 2020), Identity Politics and Its Impact on Public Passion for Digital Marketing, Interview by Daniel Solomon

escalating ethnic tensions resulting in damage to property, interruption of the teaching-learning process and, sadly, a risk to a student's life (Adamu, 2019). The ethnic-based federal system that has been cultivated for more than 25 years and the politicization of ethnicity are at the root of these problems (Hailu, 2020).

During this turmoil, social media has proved itself a double-edged sword in Ethiopia: It's capable of filling a need for more information due to limited press freedom and frequent blanket shutdowns of mobile internet, but also of pushing the country toward even greater calamity (Jeffrey, Social media users in America are stoking Ethiopia's ethnic violence, 2019). Successive waves of emigration during decades of tumult in Ethiopia have formed a worldwide Ethiopian diaspora of around two million people.

The largest communities are in the US, with estimates varying from 250,000 people to about one million (Jeffrey, Social media users in America are stoking Ethiopia's ethnic violence, 2019). By using opposition contacts in Ethiopia, a growing diaspora movement of writers, bloggers, journalists, and activists have flooded Twitter and Facebook with news sources that, they say, contradict inaccurate accounts pushed out by Ethiopia's mostly state-run media or by muddled foreign reporters.

This, in turn, troubled the government to the point that it started to take the internet down across the nation. At least 22 African states have partially or fully blocked the internet or obstructed social media networks in the past five years due to a political uprising (Dahir, Ethiopia's tech startups are ready to run the world, but the internet keeps getting blocked 2019). For instance, it has jammed the Internet following days of protests and unease that resulted in deaths and injuries in universities and towns across the East African nation (Latif, 2017).

This political instability has impacted online businesses all over the country. In the capital of Addis Ababa, business owners and journalists believe the fact that they were using VPNs to connect to the internet and access messaging platforms (Hailu, 2020). Some business owners complained that they have been struggling to get online to book travel plans for their clients due to the internet restrictions (Samuel, Ethiopia has been offline, and nobody knows why, 2019).

Still were Some who were forced to shut down their Internet cafes, while others were unable to do their respective online business (Gizaw, 2020). The number of people who appealed to have considerably lost the degree of their passion for digital marketing despite its lucrativeness and other multiple advantages is quite significant.

2.3. The Advancement of Technology and Digital Marketing

The world economy is being reshaped by an even newfangled quicker wave of technologies, driven by innovations in telecommunications, computing, and the global information networks (Marmer, 2018). Likewise, digitalization is also rapidly spreading the very factors of production technology, information, and ideas that make economic advances possible (Stefen, 2018). It seems we are entering a new era, in which a series of innovations that leverage the internet could have a major impact on trade costs and international trade.

The Internet of things, artificial intelligence, 3D printing, and Blockchain have the potential to profoundly transform the way we trade, who trades, and what is traded (Yi, 2018). Such advancements in digital technologies can also bring about changes in the structure of the trade.

Beyond easing trade in goods, digital technologies can facilitate services trade and enable new services to emerge (Blanke, 2016). Some even think the fact that the Internet has not only contributed towards making life easy, but it has also changed the mode and style of life for many. The number of people springing quite a significant amount of time on the Internet can tell swift change (Gizaw, 2020).

The impact of digital technology on global trade has attracted public attention worldwide with the discussions mainly focused on online sales (Escsp, 2019) states that the. The rising importance of digital marketing was already noted by international organizations in the late 1990s. For example, in 1999, UNCTAD stated that "electronic commerce has the potential to be a major engine for trade and development on the global scale" (UNCTAD, 1999, p. 1).

In the health sector, for instance, AI-enabled frontier technologies are helping to save lives, diagnose diseases and extend life expectancy (Shaping our future together, 2020). Likewise, in education, virtual learning environments and distance learning have opened programs to students who would otherwise be excluded.

WTO work in the same period stated that the value of electronic commerce has catapulted from virtually zero to a predicted $300 billion in the 10 years up to the turn of the century (WTO, 1998, p. 1). The turn of the 20th century is considered by many as the first wave of globalization (Lynch, 2019), and the introduction of faster and more reliable steam ships was credited for much of the world trade boom of the time.

Other technological developments, such as the standardization of shipping containers in the middle of the century, have also played a pivotal role in the history of international trade (Lynch, 2019). The fourth industrial revolution, driven by rapid technological change and digitalization, has already had a profound impact on global trade, economic growth, and social progress.

Cross-border e-commerce has generated trillions of dollars in economic activity in recent years and continues to accelerate. In short, technological advances in the past few decades have greatly increased the competitive nature of the economic business world (Habas, 2018). The ability of data to move across borders underpins new business models, boosting global GDP by 10% in the last decade alone (Def, 2019).

In support of the advancement of digital marketing and its impact on the world economy today (Kallmer, 2019) says digital technology drives global commerce. It ensures payments happen on time and in the right amount. It keeps farms yielding abundantly, factories working efficiently, and trucks running smoothly. It allows stores to track and manage inventory seamlessly.

Online businesses must follow the same legal requirements as businesses with physical locations. However, they have quite several differences when it comes to their respective functionalities. Hence, to grow and thrive in the modern economy online businesses need trade rules that protect their operations and address today's digital reality (Kallmer, 2019).

All of the above-mentioned literature underscores the fact that there is a tremendous development of technology observed in recent past years. The progress is still in continuous and uninterrupted advancement. Such an improvement has made a significant impact on the digital world in general and digital marketing. The impact of the advancement of this technology is felt across the world to the point that such marketing has reached the highest level of leading the world economy (Blanke, 2016).

This research goes along with the findings of the above works. It uses them as input to support its results and conclusions. It has also instigated the said findings to exhibit the danger of the digital divide that would ensue if Ethiopia is not able to curve the identity politics to idea poetics as soon as it could.

2.4. Internet Penetration in Ethiopia

Ethiopia exists in large pockets of no network zones (Ethiopia's internet penetration less than half the African average, 2020). There were only 21.14 million internet users in Ethiopia at the beginning of 2020 (DigitalL 2020: Ethiopia, 2020) which is less than 0.1percent of the world's Internet users. According to the same data portal, in that same year, Internet penetration in the country was only 19 percent which is less than half the African average. There were 6.20 million social media users in Ethiopia in January 2020 (DigitalL 2020: Ethiopia, 2020). In rural areas and 4G is only available in the capital (Ethiopia Internet Users, 2020).

Having more than 60 percent of its population under the age of 30 and less than 25 percent of its population having access to the Internet, connecting, and expanding the Internet would have been a key part of Ethiopia's Government strategy to tackle several of its acute social problems[23]. Ethiopians are not yet benefiting from the many Internet-related services that other countries must develop their economies as well as to improve the lives of their people[24].

---

[23] Cyrus Hailu (January 12, 2020), Identity Politics and Its Impact on Public Passion for Digital Marketing, Interview by Daniel Solomon

[24] Mesfin Kassa (January 12, 2020), Identity Politics and Its Impact on Public Passion for Digital Marketing, Interview by Daniel Solomon

The advent of ethnic federalism that politicized tribal identity has produced both intended and unintended outcomes. While arguably easing large-scale ethnic conflicts, it has led to local socioeconomic disputes and sharper inter-ethnic and intra-ethnic divides, often to the disadvantage of historically marginalized groups (Lovise, The politics of ethnicity in Ethiopia: Actors. power and mobilization under ethnic federalism, 2011).

In reaction to the outcome of such an identity-based exclusive politics round of protests has started erupting here and there all over the nation (Abdu, 2019). Using certain social media such as Twitter and Facebook political activists from around the world callously persisted in inciting and galvanizing protestors to upheaval the rule (Kelecha, 2018). Such media lived beyond the country's restrictive censorship and were instrumental to changing the country's political tyranny (Feigenbaum, 2018).

By and large, violence and protest started to break out everywhere remonstrating against the ruling party demanding social justice, political reforms, and the rule of law (LAROK, 2019). Using social media, political activists from around the world callously persisted inciting and galvanizing protestors to upheaval the rule (Kelecha, 2018). In return, the regime has singled out social media as being a key factor in driving the unrest now gripping the country (Schemm, 2016), (Ethiopia imposes state of emergency as unrest intensifies, 2016) and (Diffrent, 2017).

To slow down the political turmoil, social media has been cut off by the sitting regime (Feigenbaum, 2018). What's more, it persistently blocked the Internet across the nation (Ambaye, 2019), (Ademo, 2012), and (Abdu, 2019). Such obstruction of access to the Internet has happened multiple times against the rights of the citizens for information.

The government does care as such to give due heads and cares even for such basic human rights if there is a political commotion shaking the country at any rate. Besides the régime does not give the impression to invest any better in the expansion of the Internet and digitalization across the nation (Latif, 2017) and (Economics, 2019).

According to some sources, it does not either allocate an adequate budget in the field (Evans, 2012) or inspire private investors to get into the area. Instead, it keeps them away from investing in ICT-related endeavors including but not limited to digital marketing by discouraging them with a shortage of hard currency and too much taxation (ESAT, 2017).

On top of all these, the implementation of a continuous Internet shutdown by the government (Admin, 2019), and the state monopoly of the Internet industry (Aden, 2018) might drive the country to vanish into the sands of the digital divide. In general, the Internet is not as available as expected. The great majority of the country has no or little coverage (Lema, 2019).

Even in the places where the Internet is available, it does not seem affordable to most of the inhabitants especially for those who are leading a kind of hand-to-mouth life (Mersha, 2019). Passed the said challenges, at the time people suffer from internet outages and blockages. The outage could be caused by a power outage, while the outage has to do with the government that shuts down the internet for political motives (Hailu, 2020).

2.5. The Internet: Impact on World Politics

The purpose of this part of the review is to highlight how the internet is impacting the politics of the current world and by so doing why some countries like Ethiopia that run ethnic-based federalism tend to shut down the internet to cool down their political instability. As many tend to agree the Internet is one example of the diffusion of technology. Much like other technologies, the Internet has diffused unevenly across countries, raising concerns over a digital divide.

Conferring to the proposition by (Milner, 2006) the spread of internet diffusion has been driven by neither technological nor economic factors alone. Rather, political factors exert a powerful influence. (Milner, 2006) and (Shelley, 2006) believe the fact that groups that believe they will lose from the Internet use political institutions to enact policies that block the spread of the Internet.

Some political institutions make this easier than others. According to them, data from roughly 190 countries from 1991 to 2001 show that a country's regime type matters greatly, even when controlling for other economic, technological, political, and sociological factors. In their findings, they have clearly stated that democratic governments facilitate the spread of the Internet relative to autocratic ones. Thus, the spread of democracy may help reduce the digital divide (Norris, 2017).

The countries such as Ethiopia where the lack of democracy is rampant the spread of the Internet can hardly be well. Almost half of all governments can be considered undemocratic, there is a seldom rule of law, unfortunate justice, and biased political system[25]. Trends in a democracy are analyzed for all countries worldwide since the early 1970s. The finding underscores those political institutions crafted on the top of debauched governments such as identity-based exclusive politics would not work very much towards the development of democracy at any given rate.

Menu, Jay D. Hmielowski, and Myiah J. Hutchens (Article Menu, 2018) in their article entitled "Democratic Digital

---

[25] Cyrus Hailu (January 12, 2020), Identity Politics and Its Impact on Public Passion for Digital Marketing, Interview by Daniel Solomon

Inequalities: Threat and Opportunity in Online Citizenship from Motivation and Ability" have noted the fact that internet access provides several ways to read, share, and discuss politics. Guided by research on digital inequalities, opportunities motivation, ability framework, and communication gaps, they have found that Internet skill and political interest, but not education, are related to greater online news reading and sharing.

Over the past decade, political discussions have migrated from water coolers and dinner tables to smartphones and social media. Some years back, candidates had no Internet platforms to express their views and proposals online. By then, things were drastically different. Now, social media such as Twitter, Instagram, and Facebook have transformed the way candidates interact with their constituencies (Leetaru, 2020).

People talk to each other in their way using these social media. Many tend to agree on the influence of the Internet on politics. three sites have Some even go further to say, Twitter, Instagram, and Facebook have become almost indispensable staples of the modern state, used by elected officials up to world leaders to communicate with their domestic citizenry and audiences abroad (Hailu, 2020).

2.6. The Internet: Impact on Ethiopian Politics

There is a concern that information and communication technologies (ICTs), which are expected to contribute to the development of all humans, actually widen the inequalities between the developed world and the underdeveloped world, the rich and poor, whites and blacks, the educated and less-educated, etc., creating the so-called "digital divide" (Min, 2010).

The democratic divide could raise a critical social question since it suggests that there may be politically marginalized people in the digital world. This happens in many ways than it is possible to list down each one of them here.

According to some scholars in the field, if properly used the Internet can contribute to democracy by bonding people, regardless of territory, and by creating public spheres and new social movements (Rheingold, 1993). Many studies such as (Hill, 2005) and (Ott, 2000) have shown how citizens use computers and the Internet for enhanced political and democratic initiatives.

Nevertheless, if used for a different purpose such as opposing the government, social violence, and political upheaval, they might end up frantically with the random incarceration, torture, and death of some of the inciters. In this regard, some scholars and writers reflect that the internet is one of the biggest risks and challenges to the formation of democracy most importantly in developing countries (Cao, 2014) and (Article Menu, 2018).

According to them democracy and hate speech, privacy breaches, or government-sponsored hacking might come to mind (Dealatorre, 2019). They think the fact that the lack of political will is one of the major barriers creating the digital divide. This divide signifies the differences between those who do and do not, use the panoply of digital resources to engage, mobilize, and participate in public life.

The existence of the democratic divide, to any extent, poses an important social question. Under the concept of the democratic divide, according to Norris, the Internet mainly serves to reinforce the activism of the activists, facilitating participation for those who are already interested in politics. That is what has happened in the recent Ethiopian identity-based exclusive politics lead by EPRDF.

We got to have quite a several activists online running opposition politics against the power in office and as a result, the society got to be involved quite significantly. As society turns out to be progressively reliant on e-commerce, governmental and social barriers may get to be compounded. As non-electronic voices are marginalized from political participation the pressure might go up to the point of paralyzing the office of the government.

Hence, the office continued crafting laws and rules to officially ban citizens from using the Internet for political purposes. Many were put to detained, killed, and murdered for this cause. Speaking about this fact (Shaban, 2019) says the current government continues to dismantle repressive laws that in the past led to mass jailing of journalists, activists, and opponents. Nevertheless, the digital fight went on and the ruling EPRDF lost a war of information and was forced to reform in the wake of unrelenting protests and online activism.

The essential feature of plural or multicultural society is its ability to protect the unity of the society and avoiding tensions, violence, or chaos without denying the identities of its building blocks. Such basic ingredients of a multiethnic and diverse society have been damaged within the last three decades in Ethiopia.

The negative political narrative which designates Amhara as an oppressor over the rest of the ethnicities in the country was able to erode the good relationship citizens had among themselves. Instead, they started to perceive each other as adversaries and antagonists. Following this, discrimination, displacement, ethnic clearance, and mass assassination, became rampant on an everyday basis all over the country (Latif, 2017).

Various ethnic groups in Ethiopia have very recently been subjected to forced internal displacement, in what are still unfolding and complex tragedies (Abate, 2015). Millions of people were forced to leave their homes each year because of artificial disasters, armed conflict, or other man-made plights caused by identity politics (Ademo, 2012). The country now has nearly three million new internally displaced people because of ethnic and communal conflict (Diaz, 2019).

With more than eighty ethnic groups, tensions between peoples have been a repeated theme in Ethiopian history, leading to a constant strain being placed on its citizens and the state. In short, the future of the country is now threatened by the tragic collapse of rule of law, stemming from an upsurge in ethnic violence and displacement (Ambaye, 2019). The displaced in Ethiopia are now living in inhumane conditions, crowded into cramp shelters, often with no home to return to (Mbah, 2009).

Most of these displacement and mass massacres have been targeting figure-counted ethnic groups with Amhara being the number one target (Samuel, Ethiopia has been offline, and nobody knows why, 2019). As indicated above, nearly, all these assaults were triggered by social media. (Aldonas, 2015). The use of social media in politics including Twitter, Facebook, and YouTube has dramatically changed the game in Ethiopian politics (Assefa, 2019).

For instance, at least over eighty people were killed following political unrest caused by a Facebook post on the killing of Hachalu Hundessa, a popular protest singer, who died at the hands of unknown assailants. Without such social media, the political ills which were triggered by the death of the singer would have minimal visibility.

Such vigor and violence, in effect, have shifted the political mind and perspective of the regime from offering limited access to the total prohibition of the Internet services all over the country at least during the times of the violence. Every time there is violence, public opposition, or any demonstration against the sitting government, there is a suspension of the internet (Gizaw, 2020).

The embargo sparked anger and frustration among citizens like access to social media platforms was blocked (Hailu, 2020). Consequently, the violence gets going, people get killed, displaced, and persecuted, exhibiting, how digital technology affects democracy works by influencing political mobilization and amplifying political polarization, changing the tools of government (Gilardi, 2016).

In short, digital technology along with social media had had a profound political impact on contemporary Ethiopia (Gilardi, 2016) and (Farrell, 2012). They have played an increasingly important role in influencing the political processes of the country to the worst (Farrell 2012). Hence, some governments might mislay their interest to expand ITC services and their availability even at a policy level within the control of their respective country for fear political shakiness might arise.

2.7. The Internet: Impact on Ethiopian Economy

The purpose of this review is not to statistically prove how the Internet has impacted the Ethiopian economy positively or otherwise. Instead, it assumes a position of forming a theoretical premise as to how the Internet could influence the economy given the political atmosphere is not doing well as the cause seems in current Ethiopia. There were past studies that confirmed the positive relationship between the Internet and economic growth (Bongo, 2005).

These studies suggest that ICTs have the potential in alleviating poverty in poor countries. These technologies have also been viewed by governments and international aid agencies as important tools for national integration because they are capable of enabling greater access to health and education services, and creating economic opportunities for underprivileged population groups (Jensen, 2007); (Mercer, 2007) and (Oberski, 2004).

The '2006 Information and Communications for Development' report published by The World Bank (2006) considered ICTs to be crucial to poverty reduction. Jensen's (2007) micro-level study on fishermen in Kerala shows that the adoption of mobile phones can promote economic and social welfare not only for these fishermen but also for consumers.

This study implies that poverty alleviation in one sector can have a positive spillover effect for other individuals in the supply value chain or other sectors within the economy. There were also other reported cases in which wireless communications technologies were observed to have generated benefits for communities. For example, villages in Robib, Cambodia, were reported to have leapfrogged from an agricultural to an information economy through wireless networks (radio, 2006).

The villagers were able to access medical and health services and the global marketplace for their cottage industry through wireless communications technology. In Africa, it was found that information available using mobile phones enabled farmers in Senegal to double the prices of their crops and herders in Angola to locate their cattle through GPS (global positioning system) technology. If such benefits can be harnessed from strategic applications of ICTs in each economic sector, it may be translated into economic growth and welfare gains at the national aggregate.

Developing countries are generally latecomers to the Internet revolution. If these countries emulate the adoption of ICTs, which are also being adopted in industrialized countries, they would be exposed to the same technological potentials as the developed countries would. Successful exploitation of the technological potentials by developing countries has significant implications on the narrowing of the economic gap between developed and developing countries as the latter catches up in economic development. EIU's study (2004) highlighted a crucial point for harnessing positive effects from ICTs application for developing countries.

It examines the relationship between ICTs and economic growth in 26 developed countries and 34 less-developed countries between 1995 and 2002 and reported strong evidence of a positive association between ICTs and economic growth for developed countries but not for developing countries. This study attributed the weak association, in the latter group of countries, to the absence of a critical mass in the Internet adoption, suggesting that significant economic growth will only be attained if a minimum threshold of the Internet penetration and usage is achieved.

In other words, if there is a digital divide between developed and developing countries, it is likely to result in considerable differences in economic development. Investment in ICTs and effective applications of these technologies for economic growth are likely not to be straightforward for developing countries. One of the major challenges confronting developing countries has been that investments on the Internet compete with the provision of necessities for the poor (Ochieng, 2000).

Investment in ICTs and their enabling infrastructures constitute an expensive affair for developing countries, which tend to bear a high burden of debts. In addition, such investment will involve a long pay-back period because of the nascent demand conditions in their market, which usually are weak or inadequate.

2.8. Digital Divide: Essence and Occurrence

The development of digital technologies that leverage the internet to generate, store and process data promises to transform the world economy even more. We are entering a new era in which computers, automation, and data analytics are coming together in an entirely new way. Such new technologies may decrease the relevance of distance, whether geographical, linguistic, or regulatory. They also facilitate searches for products, help to verify quality and reputation, and help to match consumer preferences to products (Yi, 2018).

In contrast, physical infrastructure, border processes, and geographical factors might become less relevant, which would benefit remote or landlocked economies, as well as economies with less developed physical infrastructures and customs procedures. To realize the potential benefits of digital marketing fully, an increasing number of governments have adopted digital development strategies, which encompass cross-cutting policy measures aimed at improving infrastructure, establishing an adequate regulatory framework, reducing the cost of doing business, and facilitating relevant skills development.

Both goods and services trade policies can play an important role in promoting the digital economy. Despite the evidence of the benefits of open and non-discriminatory policies and the adverse effects of restrictive policies and regulation, however, trade measures are still imposed by some governments to protect local businesses, including digital platforms, from foreign competition, restricting the access and operation of foreign services suppliers.

Governments are also developing and implementing new rules and regulations in the pursuit of public policy objectives such as data privacy, cyber security, or consumer protection. Such efforts of governments all around the world would enhance the far-reaching advances in information and communications technologies (ICTs) in tandem with the globalization of trade, investment, business regulation, production, and consumption have signaled the rise of informational capitalism (Parayil, 2007).

On the contrary, there are those other governments that exhibit poor interest in advancing social networks and digitalization. Due to demotic political upheavals, some governments go to the extent of banning and blocking the internet across their respective nations. To mention some but few, Ethiopia blocks internet access to cool down the internal unrest caused by identity-based exclusive politics that the country runs. For instance, recently there was an internet outage in Ethiopia due to political reasons.

An internet shutdown has been in force across Ethiopia since Saturday, after a group of soldiers staged a failed coup in Amhara state, the birthplace of many of Ethiopia's emperors as well as its national language, Amharic. (Mbah, 2009). Such situations could result in a digital divide, which is a phenomenon linked not only to the topic of access to the Internet but also to the one of usage and usage benefit (Fuchs, 2008). The digital divide refers to the separation between those who have access to digital information and communications technology (ICT) and those who do not (Riggins, 2005).

It began to gain popularity when it became a mainstream political topic in the US in the 1990s. And eventually, it achieved recognition as an English colloquial term in dictionaries such as 'The Australian Concise Oxford Dictionary 4th edition' and 'The Penguin English Dictionary 2nd edition'. Although the term 'digital divide' has taken on a broader and more cavernous meaning than 'information gap', there have been times that the latter was used synonymously with the former.

The digital divide is conceivably a profound equivocal term (Gunkel, 2003). Based on the idea it might designate, quite a range of implications. At times, it could suggest a plain border between two patently divided groups with a sound gap among them (KUMAR, 2019), a gap that has to do with skills caused by passions to ICT, cultural perspectives, and/or other social dogmas which includes but not limited to political ideologies and perspectives (Park, 2018).

It could also indicate a sort of generational divide in digital awareness (Akl, 2014). Technological innovation is reshaping the world and putting new tools in the hands of people everywhere (Klein, 2014). Nonetheless, technology for some older demographics is a source of fear and insecurity (Smith, 2014). They seem to be late adopters to the world of technology compared to their younger compatriots, at times even getting cut off from the arena (Rainie J. A., 2018).

The digital divide could also signify the difference between individuals with and without access to technology (Lura, 2015), a sort of absolute inequality. According to (van Dijk, 2002) most of such inequalities in the access to digital technology are more of a relative kind and can easily be worked out if there is the will to reverse it.

However, in all cases, people that do not use digital technology are missing many opportunities (Lentz, 2002). If proper attention is not given to them before it is too late to fill the gap, they even might be excluded from future society (van Dijk, 2002). It still must be demonstrated that such people cannot live as normal citizens in current modern society without using digital technology (Abelow, 2020).

The digital divide could occur due to a sort of segregating, partial, and prejudicial political ideologies (Dijk, 2018). Current Ethiopia is one of the countries which exercises such political creeds as a directorial principle (Amanda Onion, 1991), ever since the Ethiopian Peoples' Revolutionary Democratic Front (EPRDF) came to office after toppling the Derg military junta in 1991 (Getachew Y. Y., 2019). The regime has distorted the stable centralized government into nine fragmented federal states (Taye B. A., 2019).

It did this by introducing jingoistic exclusive political thought and dichotomizing citizens according to their respective ethnic profiles (Gebreluel, 2019). In other words, as in the Soviet Union, every piece of land in Ethiopia was inscribed as the ethnic homeland of a particular group, constitutionally dividing the population into a permanent majority alongside permanent minorities with little stake in the system.

The digital divide typically exists between those in cities and those in rural areas; between the educated and the uneducated; between socioeconomic groups; and, globally, between the more and less industrially developed nations (Rouse, 2019). As the availability of the Internet is used to create, alter, maintain, and reproduce existing social systems, its paucity might cause the existence of a digital divide.

Even among populations with some access to technology, the digital divide can be evident in the form of lower-performance computers, lower-speed wireless connections, lower-priced connections such as dial-up, and limited access to subscription-based content. However, this research will focus only on those aspects of the digital divide that resulted in less or no availability of internet access in the country.

The impact of this digital divide would not be easy. It might cut off such countries from the globalization truck and set them aside all alone. Digital marketing is an important part of the world economy - and the movement of data across borders is now a central feature of globalization (Francesca, 2019). It is, therefore, critical for the health of the world economy, and the prospect of economic growth in all countries, that markets are open to the movement of digital goods, services and investment, Internet professionals, and data. Such governments that if they don't take due action in the due time, they might be forced to embrace the consequences of staying aloft from digitalization.

The cost is not going to be that easy. Recent estimates suggest that the potential economic growth to be realized from liberalizing barriers to Internet access and digital marketing across the G20 could be as much as US$4.2 trillion, and this potential is even greater for the developing world, where a combination of growing youth-aged populations, rising incomes, and urbanization will reduce the marginal cost of extending access to a wider population in the period immediately ahead (Aldonas, 2015).

2.9. Country Level Political Risk

In a broader sense, country-level political risk is the degree to which either a political or economic unrest or both affect the securities apparats of a country to do business be it online or otherwise (Wagner, 2016). It signifies the likelihood of a country being less attractive to invite business ventures because of economic or political disruptions (Kauffman, 2017).

The political upheavals could emanate from the internal dissensions and instabilities within a given country. External factors could also contribute a great deal in this regard (Daniel, 2012). For instance, issues related to global trade will continue, resulting in persistent political and economic uncertainty for businesses (Alexander, 2017).

Therefore, country-level political risk comprises the various risks triggered by internal or external causes affecting the expansion of both local and foreign investment. In other words, it is a sort of uncertainty that makes the probability of investing within a given country dubious. This risk would also affect the advancement of technology and by so doing Internet penetration and digital marketing[26].

There are three types of country-level political risk: sovereign risk, economic risk, and political risk (Conrow, 2017). This paper is much interested in the third type of risk. Political risk could be seen from various perspectives and theories (Wagner, 2016). For this study political risk, is any risk associated with a loss of an already endowed endeavor of any given business or the absence of interest to invest in each country due to the political situations of that given country (Thakur, 2020).

Country-level political risk can be assessed and measured (Conrow, 2017). An effective country-level political risk assessment requires an evaluation of such factors as political stability, financial stability, economic outlook, and exposure to corruption. Of all these factors, political stability is a primary concern. This is so because, without due political stability, it would not be easy to do business at any rate. If a country has very good political stability, it can help a significant investment turn out (Deloach, 2017).

The turmoil in the Middle East has demonstrated that once governments undertake confiscatory or discriminatory actions, mobs take to the streets or civil war breaks out, which leads to political instability. Such instabilities usually end up paralyzing the chances of attracting business both internally and from abroad. Likewise, the pressing political situation in Ethiopia resulting from identity politics seems to hinder investment in folds than it is possible to think about it.

---

[26] Sara Solomon (January 12, 2020), Identity Politics and Its Impact on Public Passion for Digital Marketing, Interview by Daniel Solomon

2.10. Theoretical Framework

The growing rise of the Internet and other technological advances have greatly transformed how products and services are produced, distributed, and traded around the world. In this regard, digital marketing has been developing in a significant manner impacting the global economy. Such changes have boosted the efficiency, accuracy, and security of digital trading with varying impacts on the economic growth of many nations around the world.

The impact of digital trading in 2016 was estimated to be $4.2 trillion, making it the equivalent of the fifth-largest national economy in the U.S. (Digital Trade and U.S. Trade Policy, 2019). China, whose digital economy has expanded rapidly in recent years, accounts for over 40% of global transactions, and the penetration of digital trading (in percent of total retail sales) stands now at 15%, compared to 10% in the U.S. (Chen, 2019).

These technological developments could unlock numerous opportunities for individuals, entrepreneurs, and businesses around the world. However, such an advance by itself does not correspondingly guarantee stable digital marketing development or economic assimilation across nations (Yi, 2018).

An auspicious political environment along with pro-technology leadership that can manage the instantaneous technology-driven structural changes is vibrant for comparable returns. In fact, over the past two centuries, the absence of an unshakable and well-established executive political milieu has been observed to considerably pause technological expansion within the realm. Ethiopia, an emblem of freedom for the blacks, that suffers from identity-based exclusive politics for the last three decades, seems to fall under the category of these nations, impeding digital trading due to bad politics that perpetrates injustice and drought of democracy.

The shutdown of the internet at the end of June 2019, in response to deadly protests over the murder of a prominent musician, cost the Ethiopian economy at least $100 million (Mebewa, 2020). According to some reports with lower levels of Internet access, the average estimated GDP impacts amount to $6.6 million and $0.6 million per 10 million populations for medium and low Internet connectivity economies, respectively (The economic impact of disruptions to Internet connectivity, 2016).

It is possible to infer the fact that the development of digital marketing is inversely proportional to racially constructed political ideology. Which has been underway for the last thirty solid years. In other words, when the pressure of such ethnically built political creed which uses internet outage and intimidation and coercion of users by the security apparatus of the government, decreases at the rate of x, the rate of the expansion of digital marketing increases at the rate of y.

> y is inversely proportional to x
> y is directly proportional to 1/x
> *y α k/x   where:*
>> x is the rate corrupt politics decreases.
>> y is the rate digital marketing increases.
>> k is the constant of proportionality.

The hyperbola graph underneath exhibits the relationship between ethnically constructed political ideology which has been running Ethiopia for the last thirty years versus the rate of the expansion of digital trading with the constant proportion k = 20. They are inversely proportional. Such variables are those in which one variable decreases with the increase in another variable and one variable increases with the decrease in another variable. It is opposite to direct proportion.

The growth of one variable causes the decline of the other. The two variables can't grow together or otherwise. Instead, they are directly proportional to the reciprocal of each other. It means that the two quantities behave opposite. In other words, the two variables are varying inversely. In other words, they do not grow or decline equally.

Figure 1. Racial Politics vs Expansion Digital Marketing

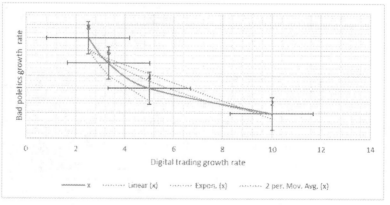

The above graph states that y which stands for bad politics is inversely proportional to x which signifies the advance of digital marketing. It also states that x is inversely proportional to y. Therefore, digital marketing cannot have a growth in countries where the political milieu is not auspicious due to instability, lack of democracy, or any other pertinent factor that could hamper the development.

The identity-based exclusive political setting in Ethiopia is reflected as bad politics manifested by three key variables: inadequate availability, indigent accessibility, and less affordability of the Internet. Thus, identity politics hurts the growth of digital marketing. The study hypothesizes the longer identity politics stays vigorous in office, the higher the probability would be for the digital divide to take place in Ethiopia which might lead the nation to a country-level political risk.

Chapter Three

METHODOLOGY

RESEARCH IS ESSENTIALLY A SYSTEMATIC procedure of finding solutions after a methodical analysis of the situational factors involved in the creation and manifestation of a given problem (Bodla, 2018). It is a springboard for any scientific study to transpire. The statement of the problem that has given birth to this research is the practice of ethnic-based politics in Ethiopia. The exercise of this practice is supposed to halt the expansion of ICT in the country, get the development of digital marketing obstructed, and probably pave the way for the digital divide.

Dependable data has been collected to accurately assess, analyses, and discourse this problem. The data has abetted explaining the variations and doubts concerning the relevance and the application of the findings of the study. Knowing the quality of research data depends on the way the informants were selected and how the data was collected, the study has polished a research procedure discussed herein under four key parts.

The first three consecutive parts discuss the research instrumentation plan, research sample size population, and research data type and collection procedures, respectively.

Primary data has been collected through questionnaires, focused group discussions, and interview with selected informants scientifically. Secondary data has also been composed of related literature, documents, and reports. The last part talks about the tools used to analyze and synthesize the data.

Daniel B. Solomon

3.1. Instrumentation Plan

This research was launched with an instrumentation plan in place. The plan embarrasses the various decisions that needed to be made even before the study was commenced. These decisions are made to determine, what data are needed to answer the research questions, how to gather the data when to gather the data, where to gather the data, and how to analyze the data. These decisions must be made as part of the instrumentation plan for the study. The plan helped guide the progress of the study to the goal of gathering data and formulating conclusions to answer the research questions.

Hence, the plan was significant to systematize and organize the roadmap of the research work. It has reinforced the various segments of the research work starting from preparing the questionnaire to defending the findings of the research passing thru the ensuing nine phases as shown on the *instrumentation* plan below.

Figure 2. Instrumentation Plan

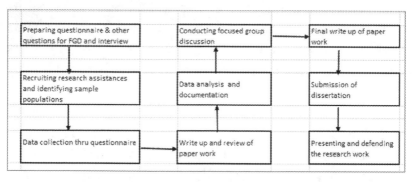

As seen above the research started with the review of related literature and other relevant readings, writing the research proposal, and preparing the research questions for conducting primary data collection thru questionnaires, focused group discussion, and interviews with selected groups.

Then, using GPower an attempt has been made to decide the sample size statistically applicable to the study. Then, the data collection activity commenced with dispatching the questionnaire to a total of 45 informants who were selected from Addis Ababa, Ethiopia. Of these informants, five of them were arbitrarily selected for both focused group and interview discourses.

The instrumentation plan has pigeonholed as to what data should be collected, when and how it should be collected, who should collect the data, and how the data is supposed to be processed and analyzed. It has also specified the steps needed to properly address the research questions and by so doing achieve the objective of the study. These, all together, had sustained the research to be well decontaminated, structured, and organized to the end. In short, the plan had given the research a well-defined clean process along with a feasible target and outcome.

3.2. Sample Size

Sampling is the act of selecting a subset of the population of interest to gain information about the entire population. A good sample size is a sort of descriptive representation of the population. Given the population of Ethiopia, the country selected for this particular study, is extensively immense, conducting scientific research on data to be assembled from the intact populace might be neither feasible nor attainable. Hence, due attention has been given to determine the population size with the help of power.

3.2.1. Sample Size Calculation

Since true inferences about the population would be made from the results obtained from the sample size, sample calculation must be done wisely and cautiously (Nayak, 2010). However, there is a growing sample size calculation concern overwhelming the scientific community (Fonseca J. F., 2014) and (Bhalerao, 2010). Such concerns are utterly reasonable; samples should not be either too big or too small since both have limitations that can compromise the conclusions drawn from the study. On the other hand, any error made in the sample size calculation might significantly affect the outcome of the study.

In this research, however, the sample size calculation was dependent on the Type I error rate. The significance level which is also known as alpha or the Type I error rate is the probability of rejecting H0 when it is true. In this regard, the smaller the Type I error rate is, the larger the sample size is required for the same power. Likewise, the smaller the Type I error rate is, the smaller the power would be for the same sample size. This is the trade-off between the reliability and sensitivity of the test.

The sample size was determined using a t-test for means difference form consistent (one sample case) on GPower with a default effect size d of 0.5, error probability of 0.05, and a power of 0.95. As shown in the chart below, the sampling distribution is denoted by a dotted blue line, while the population distribution by a solid red line. A red shaded area delineating the probability of a Type 1 error, a blue area the type 2 error, and a pair of green lines demarcating the critical points t are marked.

Figure 3. Sample Size Graph

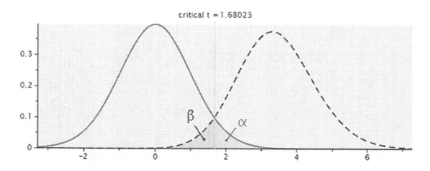

To test the hypothesis of this research at the default none certainty parameter of 3.3541020, circuit t of 1.6802300, Df of 44, a significance level of 0.05, and actual power of 0.9512400, GPower endorsed a total sample size of 45 informants.

3.2.2. Sample Size Formation

Sampling, which is selecting a subset of the population of interest to gain information about the entire population, has been taken as the most essential aspect of planning the data collection effort of this particular study. A good sample will therefore be representative of the population. The design for a sample, however, varies greatly depending on the time, money, and staff available, the logistical challenges encountered, and the intended use of the data.

To be selected to participate as an informant in this research, three criteria were set. First, the informant must be Ethiopian either by birth or law. Next, he/she must be 18 -68 years old. What is more, the informants must voluntarily take part in the research. Thus, by default, the research has intentionally left out minors and senior people principally because they are not in the active workforce group by the standing rule of law in Ethiopia which prohibits minors from participating in.

Last, the informants were required to be college graduates so that they might have a clear picture of the purpose and drive of the research. The informants happen to have the first, second, and tertiary level of degrees, which has assisted the study gain consistent data with better precision and correctness.

It has also streamlined the research work in a couple of ways. First, it has narrowed the scope of the study from a very large population of nearly 7 million people to a handy and manageable size, which kept the researcher focused, organized, and well regulated. It has also helped identify the right group of informants to the outcome of the research would apply at the end of the day.

Therefore, a team of 45 ardent informants coming from both gender groups, different religious backgrounds, three top academic levels, and good experience in digital marketing has been designed. Of them, nine and three people were indiscriminately selected for focused group discussion and interview, correspondingly.

3.3. Data Type and Data Collection Procedures

Research is a novel investigation carried out to gain knowledge and understand concepts in each subject area of specialization (Monette, 2013). Therefore, the success of any operational research depends predominantly upon what data is collected and how well it is collected. This part confers the different data types used in the research along with how procedures are used to collect them.

3.3.1. Data Type

Though deciding what data to collect would depend on the types of the project (Dillard, 2019), every study includes the collection of some type of data, be it primary or secondary data (Primary data and secondary data, 2019). In this research, both quantitative and qualitative data have been acquired from a review of related literature and the sample population designated for this research.

Since qualitative data is computable and assessable, it was gathered through a questionnaire. On the other hand, the quantitative data, which is descriptive and conceptual in its very nature, was picked up from a review of related literature, documents, focused group discussion, and interview.

The qualitative data has been used to seek reasons and justifications. Hence, the questions used in this regard were investigative and are often open-ended leaving enough room for the informants to pour off their respective thoughts. Generating such quantitative data has helped in theorizations, interpretations, developing hypotheses, and initial understandings. Contrary to the qualitative data used in this research, the quantitative data has been statistically supportive to analyze data in a more structured and organized manner with measurable precision and accuracy.

This research has not encountered discrete data which can be can technically be categorical and cannot be broken down into smaller parts. Likewise, it does not contain continuous data that can be infinitely broken down into smaller parts or data that continuously fluctuate. Making sense of qualitative data can be time-consuming and expensive, the research heavenly depends on quantitative data.

3.3.2. Collection Procedures

Data collection is the process of gathering and gaging information on a variety of interests, in an established systematic fashion that enables one to answer stated research questions, test hypotheses, and evaluate the findings and outcomes. To this end, primary data has been collected predominantly using a questionnaire, focused group discussions, and in-person interviews.

3.3.2.1. The questionnaire.

A questionnaire is one of the primary data collection techniques which involves a written set of questions, which the respondents are required to answer based on their knowledge and experience with the issue concerned (Abawi, 2013), (Bhat, 2019) and (Bhalerao, 2010). The most economical data collection method can cover a wide range of informants within a reasonable time frame (Choudhrs, 2020).

The cost that has been involved in this reach was that costly. Of course, the researcher had to travel to Addis Ababa Ethiopia a couple of times to find out some volunteers that would help to galvanize the data collection process by distributing the questionnaire to randomly selected informants. Fortunately, all the costs incurred in this research were covered by Dan Technology Consultant LLC, located in Alexandria Virginia.

The questionnaire is structured in three different tiers each having two focus areas. The first tier delivers questions that try to fetch demographic information along with the skills and interests of the informants on digital trading. This helps to analyze who the informants are and how much they are interested in the digital marketing venture. This makes the finding of the research more valuable and trustworthy[27].

The second and the third tiers entail the emblematic part of the research questionnaire. Tier two conveys questions on the availability and accessibility of the Internet. On the other hand, the third tier asks about the affordability of the Internet as well as the wishes and concerns of the informants about the perspective of digital trading given along with the occurrence of the digital divide given Ethiopia stays under the rule of identity politics.

The following process flow diagram demonstrates the entire procedure of the research in a perceptible mode.

---

[27] Mesfin Kassa (septiembre 05, 2019), Online Customers Market Preference, Interview by Daniel Solomon

Figure 4. Structure of the Questionnaire

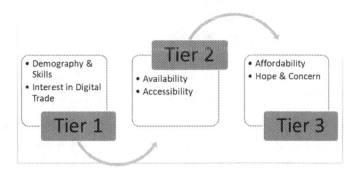

There are a total of 45 questions sorted out into the six focus areas positioned under three imperative research tiers. Figure 4.4. exhibits the percentage of the coverage of the research questions by focus areas.

Figure 5. Converge of Research Questions

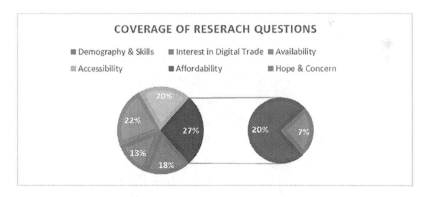

As a questionnaire believed to be the most flexible tool that ensures anonymity to its respondents (Aryal, 2019), an attempt to refrain the informants from adding their respective personal information such as name, address, and likes.

3.3.2.2. Focus group discussion.

Focus group discussion is frequently used as a qualitative approach to gain an in-depth understanding of social issues (O.Nyumba, 2018) and (Bloor, 2001). It targets to acquire data from an intentionally selected group of individuals rather than from a statistically representative sample of a broader population. In this regard, however, five of the informants in the sample size were randomly selected for focused group disunion, of them 3 were males and while the remaining two were females.

Given the rise of participatory research in conservation over the last few decades (Bennett, 2017) it is crucial to reflect on the scope and remit of focus group discussion as a methodological tool. Currently, there is relatively little or no critical discussion on the merits and demerits of focus group discussion in comparison to other similar qualitative techniques (Carey, 1994). It is, thus, very difficult to determine when and in which context, focus group discussion would be most appropriate.

Even though the application of this method in conservation research has been extensive, there is no critical assessment of the application of the technique. In addition, there are no readily available guidelines for conservation researchers (Burrows, 1997). The researcher has made every single possible effort to draft four fundamental questions for each category under tiers two and three. These questions have helped the research to better understand the intent and thought of the sample size and to draw a kind of conclusion that captures their feelings and fears.

Though some researchers have recommended a minimum of three to four group meetings for simple research topics (Burrows, 1997). After identifying convenient venues for the conversation, the researcher has conducted two focused group discussions. In both times, the conventions were held in Addis Ababa. They were so obliging, accommodating, and have created some very good handshake moments between the researcher and the informants. Since the informant was not willing to get the discussion recorded or take pictures, no footage was taken during both summits. They were both deliberately made to be camera-free.

Focus group discussion requires a team consisting of a skilled facilitator and an assistant (Kajornboon, Using interviews as research instruments, 2005). To this end, the research assistances have played a vital role. They have also helped in observing non-verbal interactions and documenting the general content of the discussion, thereby supplementing the data.

3.3.2.3. Interview.

To further understand and clarify some research questions, an interview has been conducted with two randomly selected candidates. It was a structured direct interview in the sense that the questions were pre-decided and arranged in an organized way. Apart from the follow-up questions, there were a total of four mainstream questions designed for the interview. Each of the core areas of the second and the third tires have one question attributed to each one of them. The interview was handled by the researcher himself. That has helped him to get a deeper insight into capturing the feelings and thoughts of the candidate.

Interviewing is very susceptible to a certain level of bias (O'Leary, 2004), (Mouton, 1987) and (Kajornboon, Using interviews as research instruments, 2005). In this kind of direct interview, the researcher has tried not to drive it to the direction best suiting his worldview, which may, in turn, affect the validity of results produced.

The researcher has also abstained from interpreting responses and assisting them to answer questions in such a way that it outfits his expectations, irrespective of the message the interviewee meant to put across, which has made the informants feel free and express their respective views and perspectives without any limit. In short, by adherence to research ethics, the researcher has managed to reduce bias. However, as participants were not willing to get the interview recorded for personal reasons, notes and proceedings have been taken when found important for reference and citation purposes.

3.4. Tools Used to Analyze the Research Data

To analyze the data which includes the process of filtering, organizing, and interpreting data to discover useful statistics (Khan, 2019), JAMOVIA, GPower, and excel have been implemented. Among many other research tools such as SPSS, SAS, R, Stata, JMP, and the likes, JAMOVIA is selected mainly because it is user-friendly, open-source, and has high-resolution graphs and presentations ready reports that communicate results easily and effectively.

It is intuitive to use and can provide the latest developments in statistical methodology. Besides JAMOVIA has a wide range of advanced statistical analyses that provide deeper and more meaningful insights from out of the research data. It serves as a safe space where different statistical approaches might be published side-by-side. On top of that, the researcher has a better familiarity with the tool compared to the other statistical software.

One of my interviewees who has her first degree in mathematics with a minor in statistics suggested that statistical power and sample size calculations are an important component of experimental design and are required for all research[28]. Of course, this has become a common practice in any research endeavor in the contemporary world. In this regard, GPower has been implemented. Though this tool has the potential to performs high-precision statistical power analyses for the most common statistical tests in behavioral research, in this study, it is used only to determine the sample size of the research area.

---

[28] Sara Solomon (January 12, 2020), Identity Politics and Its Impact on Public Passion for Digital Marketing, Interview by Daniel Solomon

Chapter Four

DISCUSSION AND FINDINGS

THREE VITAL TOPICS ARE ENCLOSED under this section. First, there is an ephemeral analysis of the socio-demographic characteristics and features of the sample population. Then, a comprehensive assessment has been made on the impact of ethnically constructed political ideology on the public passion for digital marketing. Finally, there is a brief discussion that unveils if the digital divide is a conceivable threat to Ethiopia, given the current political atmosphere continues to prevail.

4.1. Demographic Findings

Appropriate identification of research participants is critical to any good scientific research, particularly for assessing the results, generalizing the findings, and making comparisons in replications. (Bordens, 1996). A research article failing to report demographic variables would limit the ability of its readers to estimate whether the sample is representative of the population of interest or if procedures were adequate to carry out the research.

In the interest of fairness and fullness in the scientific research process, but more importantly, for the advancement and development of science in the ICT field, demographic discussions have been included in this discussion. Therefore, the process and outcomes of this study can be held to the standard requirements of wide-ranging scientific research reporting. Therefore, this thesis is made to have a more complete picture from which sound conclusions and references were inferred about the crux of the matter in addressing the research questions.

This part of the study has encompassed two key demographic discussions. The first part is focused on sample size distribution by age, gender, and religion, expounding in detail on the total number of the informants who have participated in the study, their numbers in terms of age, gender, and religion. The second part discusses the demography of the sample size by income level and academic preparedness, elucidating a clear picture of the informants in terms of their education and their respective annual income. Then a very brief conclusion is made on the major findings and trends observed under the topic.

4.1.1. Demography by Age, Gender, and Religion

Sample size demography by age, gender, and religion is one of the most important demographic groupings in scientific studies (Vostrikova, 2014). All the variables (age, gender, and religion) are imperative socio-demographic factors determining research outcomes and usability, particularly in descriptive studies. Such variables could also commonly help to assess certain risk factors in analytical studies (Pardeshi, 2010).

Age, gender, and religion are among the protuberant and visible demographic data that could give integrity to the findings of the mainstream of population-based studies (Bhat, 2019). Thus, this study has given due consideration to collecting and scrutinizing the age, gender, and religion of the informants.

4.1.1.1. Demography by age.

Age is a key demographic variable that helps to identify the representativeness of a particular sample population along with describing participants and providing valuable information about them to support the analysis. As evidently displayed in the JAMOVIA report below the sample size age is reported in years oscillating between 18 to 60 with a range of 42. The total valid number of informants is 45 with a missing value of 0.

The range encompasses only the active workforce age, as per the working bill of rights in Ethiopia, which considers employment starting from the age of 18 with an old-age pension settlement at the age of 60. The mean age is 37.4 while the median is 35 and the mode is 21, respectively.

The standard deviation, which suggests the dispersion of a dataset relative to its mean, is 13 years. In other words, the mainstream internet users who have the alertness to do business online arrays between 24 to 50 years of age. If we assortment this tendency to a country level most recent record where 21.14 million internet users were noted in January 2020 (Kemp, 2020), most of the citizens accessing the internet in Ethiopia might come from the aforesaid age group.

Figure 6. Sample Descriptive Frequency Table by Age

	Age
N	45
Missing	0
Mean	37.4
Median	35
Mode	21.0 [a]
Standard deviation	13.0
Range	42
Minimum	18
Maximum	60

[a] More than one mode exists, only the first is reported

Although, age could confirm a more parsimonious model in regression analyses with only one coefficient for interpretation which can identify significant trends between age and the outcome variable where they exist, for better analysis it has been categorized under five groups: 18-27, 28-37, 38-47, 48-57, and 58=<. Apart from the last age group that runs from 58 - 60, the age categories are deliberately assorted by 10 solid years. Sidestepping minors and senior citizens.

Figure 7. Frequencies of Age Group

Levels	Counts	% of Total	Cumulative %
18-27	14	31.1 %	31.1 %
28-37	11	24.4 %	55.6 %
38-47	8	17.8 %	73.3 %
48-57	7	15.6 %	88.9 %
58 =<	5	11.1 %	100.0 %

As shown in the above frequency table, the first age category (18-27) covers 26.7% of the entire sample population while the second (28-37), third (38-47), fourth (47-58), and fifth (58=<) group hold 24.4%, 17.8%, 15.6%, and 11.1%, correspondingly. This again reveals a very high concentration of participation by the younger generation as compared to the elderly ones. The subsequent pie chart provides a sort of pectoral description of the distribution of the data.

Figure 8. Frequencies Pie Chart by Age Group

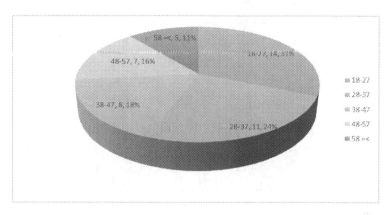

The demographic distribution below plainly indicates the fact that as age goes up participation level deteriorates, which might establish the predisposition and trend of digital marketing in terms of interest and inclination as days go by. In other words, unless otherwise, it is curved or bent by the harsh ethnic-based politics in Ethiopia, digital marketing seems to have a promising prospect in the realm as ICT progresses around the world.

Figure 9. Frequencies Bar Graph by Age Group

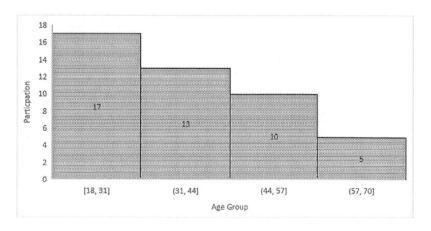

4.1.1.2. Demography by Gender.

Gender, which is a socially constructed role, behavior, and identities of female, male, and any other gender-diverse people, is often overlooked as an important demographic aspect of research both in the design and application phase of scientific reporting and communications (Gac, 2019).

It is needless to mention the fact that this oversight could potentially limit the generalizability of research findings and their applicability. Since, it influences how people perceive themselves and each other, how they behave and interact among themselves, and even the distribution of power, accesses, and resources in any given society considering gender in ICT-related fields of study is quite a necessity.

Figure 10. Frequencies of Gender

Levels	Counts	% of Total	Cumulative %
Female	23	51.1%	51.1%
Male	22	48.9%	100.0%

As seen in the report above, of a total of 45 participants 23 (48.9%) are females while 22 (51.1%) are males. Even if the questionnaire was open and appealing, there was no single informant that has expressed himself as any other gender-diverse other than the one displayed in the table.

Figure 11. Contingency Tables

Age Group						
Gender	18-27	28-37	38-47	48-57	58 =<	Total
Female	8	5	4	3		23
Male	6	6	4	4	2	22
Total	14	11	8	7	5	45

As presented in the above table both genders are disseminated into five age groups. There are a total of 14 participants in the first age groups that range from 18 to 27 years of age. Of them 8 are males and 6 are females. The second (28-37), third (38-47, fourth (48-57), and fifth (58-68) age groups, on the other hand, have 11, 8, 7, and 5 participants from both genders. Of them, 6,4,4, and 2 are males, while 5, 4, 3, and 3 females are disseminated under each age group, respectively.

4.1.1.3. Demography by Religion.

Religion has survived a period of comparative neglect and inattention even in human-focused scientific studies to become a subject matter of intense interest (Voas, 2007). However, measuring religious variables in technology-associated studies might be used to explore how religion and religiosity are associated with values, attitudes, and behavior, and allows the researcher to test theories about the causes and concerns of religious involvement in technological advancement.

In this study, an attempt has been made to investigate the religious background of the participants, so that we can have some idea as to who is better involved in digital marketing and open up questions for future studies to explore other lead questions related to the matter.

Figure 12. Frequencies of Religion

Levels	Counts	% of Total	Cumulative %
Muslim	22	48.9%	48.9%
Christian	23	51.1%	100.0%

As shown in the above graph a total of 23 and 22 informants have been observed associated with Islam and Christian religions, respectively. There was no other religion or afflation that has been chronicled by any single informant in the sample size. However, this doesn't signify the absence of other religions in the country.

According to the national census conducted in 2007, the three major religions, namely: the Ethiopian Orthodox Christians, Muslims, Protestants were reported to cover 43.5%, 33.9%, and 18.6%, respectively with 2.6% adhering to traditional dogmas (Summary and Statistical Report of the 2007 Population and Housing Census Results, 2008).

To this study, the Christen realm is put together under one category. Given the Muslim residents being less than 33.9% of the whole population in the country, according to the national census report indicated above, the fact that the Muslim making most of the participants might designate a certain trend of inclination to digital marketing and/or information technology.

4.1.2. Demography by Income and Academic Degree

The role of income and education in creating the necessary capability to access the Internet is essential. They can help improve the expansion of digital trading both in quality and quantity in many ways. They could open the doors to a wealth of information, knowledge, and resources, increasing opportunities for doing digital trading online and even beyond. This part of the study focuses discussing on the distribution of the informants according to their respective income levels and academic preparedness.

4.1.2.1. Demography by Income.

Income is one of the most significant factors that would easily impact digital marketing from both buyer and seller sides (Fayyaz, 2018). According to some research, it is only those people with enough buying and/or selling power that can be a part of digital marketing either way. In other words, the lack of sufficient earnings can restrict and curb all or some of the advantages connected with the consumption of digital marketing. Since, having a vibrant understanding of the sample population in terms of this imperative factor, due attention is offered to collecting and analyzing income-related data, which in turn has helped to arrive at a thorough conclusion, at the end.

Though Birr is the active currency in Ethiopia, for convenience's sake, the income data is calculated every year into a US exchange rate. Based on the primary income data obtained from the informants, the annual income level is pigeonholed under four categories: Income Group I, Income Group II, and Income Group III, whose annual income is > $1800.00, $1801.00 - $3000.00, $3001.00 - $5000.00, respectively.

The Income Group IV annual income is <$5001.00. The below graph exhibits the sample size distribution by income level under these categories.

Figure 13. Frequencies of Income

Levels	Counts	% of Total	Cumulative %
Income Group I	18	40.0%	40.0%
Income Group II	12	26.7%	66.7%
Income Group III	11	24.4%	91.1%
Income Group IV	4	8.9%	100.0%

18 (40.0%) informants come under Income Group I. Of these informants, the gender population is equally 50% from each group. In terms of religion, we have 12 (66.66%) Muslims while there are only 6 (33.33%) Christians, which might indicate a little about the trend of public passion towards digital marketing about religion. What is more, 8 (44.44%) informants are from the first age group (18-27), while 5 (27.77%), 4 (22.22%), and 1 (11.11%) informants are from the other three subsequent age groups. Each of the first three age groups, 18-27, 28-37, and 38-47 have a 3 (25%) distribution.

Likewise, 12 (26.7%), 11(24.4%), and 4(8.9%) informants are categorized under Income Group II, Income Group III, and Income Group IV. Of them, there are 4 (33.33%) females and 8 (66.67%) males. In terms of religion, this group has 4 (33.33%) Muslims and 8 (66.67%) Christians. Each of the first three age groups, 18-27, 28-37, and 38-47 have a 3 (25%) distribution of participants. The last two age groups (48-57, and 58<), on the other hand, have 1 (8.33%) and 2(16.66%) members, respectively.

There are 3 (27.27%) males and 8 (72.72%) females under Income Group III. Moreover, the group has 5 (45.45%) Muslims and 6 (54.54%) Christians. In terms of age group, the first two age groups (18-27 and 28-47) embrace 3 (27.27%) members each, while the other two age groups have 2 (18.18%) each.

The number of females and males is equally 2 (50%) in each group while the number of Muslims and christens in the last income groups is 1 (25%) and 3 (75%). There is no single informant from the first age group (18-27) qualifying for this income group. Nevertheless, we have 1 (25%) participant from the other four age groups.

4.1.2.2. Demography by Academic Level.

Education has enormous potential to improve the quality of life, which is one of the pillars that justifies and manifests development. As it empowers individuals to build more wealthy and successful lives and societies to achieve economic prosperity and social welfare, education also does a significant contribution to the expansion of digital trading. An effective and operative digital trading seems to have an educated staff capable of operating online business at a level where it holds a competitive advantage over the others.

Hence, trying to find out the academic level of the people involved in digital trading is worth doing it. This might exhibit if digital trading has any correlation with academic degrees. Thus, due data has been gathered from the informants on their respective academic levels. The ensuing table illustrates the distribution of this data.

Figure 14. Frequencies of Academic Level

Levels	Counts	% of Total	Cumulative %
First Degree Holders	22	48.9 %	48.9 %
Second Degree Holders	20	44.4 %	93.3 %
Third Degree Holders	3	6.7 %	100.0 %

The academic level of the informants is dealt with within three groups as First-Degree Holders, Second Degree Holders, and Third-Degree Holders. The total number of informants having the first degree is 22, which covers 48.9%, of which 44.45% are in under the first age group (18 - 27) while the second (28 - 37), third (37 - 48), fourth (48- 57) and fifth (58 - 68) age groups have 18.18%, 18.18%,13.63%, and 4,54%, correspondingly. In this group, we have 7 (38.88%) female and 11 (61.61%) male participants, while there are 10 (55.55%) Muslims and 8 (44.44%) Christians.

From the second-degree and third-degree holders, we get 20 and 3 informants each covering 44.4% and 6.7% of the whole sample population size. When seen from the perspective of the age groups. The second-degree category accounts for 4 (18.18%), 7 (31.81%), 3 (13.63%), 4 (18.18%), and 2 (9%) while the third category has 1 (4.54%) and 2 (9%) from people who age group runs 38-47 and 58 and above, respectively.

The female to the male population under the second academic group display as 14 (70%), 6 (30%), while there is an equal distribution of participants in terms of religion. The third group, on the other hand, has 2 (66.66%) females and 1 male (33.33%). The Muslim to Christen population is also 2 (66.66%) to 1(33.33%).

The most frequently appearing academic degree is First Degree Holders. However, this does not compulsorily propose a sort of trend when the academic readiness of the informant rises interest for digital exchange drops. Nonetheless, there is a clear pattern that exhibits the rise of an academic degree as the age group upturns.

4.1.2. Conclusion: Demography of the Sample Size

The above discussion gives some highlights as to who is getting involved in the digital trading ecosphere, in terms of age, gender, religion, income level, and academic degree. It also displays tendencies and trends towards the degree of participation by demographic profile. As seen in the discussion, females, and Muslims seem to get more interested in getting their hands on the digital trading world as compared to males and Christian.

When it comes to sexual orientation, even if, the questionnaire was open-ended and inclusive, there was no single informant that has claimed to have a different gender identity other than female and male. What is more, despite income level and academic degree, the younger generation seems to express better interest in digital trading than the elderly ones. In other words, as the age group goes up the passion for digital marketing seems to decline.

4.2. The Impact of Identity Politics on Public Passion to Digital Marketing

The digital world has already become a crucial component of contemporary politics (Howard, 2005). In some developed countries such as the USA, politicians use digital technologies to raise money, organize volunteers, and do opposition research.

On the contrary, in certain developing countries, such as Ethiopia the digital perspective seems to be under a recurrent embargo (Tronvoll, 2019), which, in turn, has instigated an impact on the expansion of digital trading paving the gateway for the digital divide. Hence, two key topics are enclosed in this section.

First, the assessment that deliberates on the impact of xenophobic exclusionary tribal political practice on the public passion for digital marketing. To find out this impact a total of five dependent and independent variables have been implemented. Public passion for digital marketing (PPFDT) is a dependent variable.

This is so because its value fluctuates whenever variations are detected. The independent variables encompass three important variables namely, frequency of government Internet outage (FGIO), and minimum security and safety challenge (MSSC). Thus, the independent variables have been manipulated to realize their respective impact on the dependent variables.

The study examines if the informants have adequate passion to do business on digital trading. To this end, a single question has been asked to mark the degree of passion 1-5, 5 being the best and 1 the lowest. The question was asked three times under three different conditions. The first time, it was meant to get how the informants were passionate to do digital trading if there were favorable conditions in terms of the availability and accessibility of the Internet.

The second and the third time, under the condition where there is a recurrent government, made Internet outages, and personal security and safety-related notices were encountered. The feedback gathered in particular to the first instance was used as a baseline to compare the degree of the passion of the informants collected in the second and third instances. Hence, this part of the paper discusses and analyzes the data acquired from these three questions.

4.2.1 Public Passion to Digital Marketing at the Kickoff Stage

Digital trading in today's markets can be stressful and oftentimes, traders might make arbitrary decisions in consequence (Steenbarger, 2015). Without a strong passion for the job, overcoming these pitfalls can be a difficult task (Shull, 2012). Many tend to agree on the fact that achieving in digital trading takes time, guts, the desire for hard work, and the relentless determination to take due action in due time (McCall, 2019).

In other words, though digital trading needs quite a lot of basics, which includes but not limited to, time, computer skill, investment, and the likes, to go online and do it insistently, requires strong enthusiasm and/or public passion. This does not necessarily mean everyone, whoever comes into the world of digital trading, does not come with some type of expectation. They all do. Some people see digital trading as a shortcut to wealth while others think of it as a friend-rising platform. For some, it is fun and a sort of entrainment. There could be more other people who take it entirely from a different perspective.

Be that as it may, regardless of where one comes from, one thing is certain; one can very hardly manage to do digital trading without passion for it. This has been well stressed in the focused discussion conducted with handpicked informants, seconded by all the interviews made with 5% of the informants designated for a consultation to reinforce the findings of the research. According to them, given the current intimidating and repressive political condition prevailing in Ethiopia emanating from the ethnic-based political ideology, what kept them all to be still passionate about digital trading is the passion they have built over time towards it.

Scrutinizing the level of passion, one has to digital trading at the kickoff time might serve as a baseline to measure up how the passion keeps going as other independent factors vacillate over time. Hence, to collect such a reference line data, the following question was asked to 45 informants with 0 missing value: "Given Internet is available, affordable, and accessible and there is no shortage of hard currency to do digital trading, how would you rate your passion to it 1 – 5, 5 being the best passion and 1 the least."

Figure 15. Public Passion for Digital Trading at Kickoff: Proportion Test

Level	Count	Proportion
4	12	0.267
5	33	0.733

Answering the question, the least score recorded is 4 out of 5 while the median is 5 while the mean is 4.73 which signifies the fact that the great majority of them sample size has a strong passion for digital trading at the kickoff stage. To be better precise, 33 (73.33%) of the informants appealed to have the best of passion to do digital trading while 12 (26.66%) said they have a very good passion. There was no single informant who claimed to have the first three selections (very poor, poor, and good) passion.

Figure 16. Sample Distribution

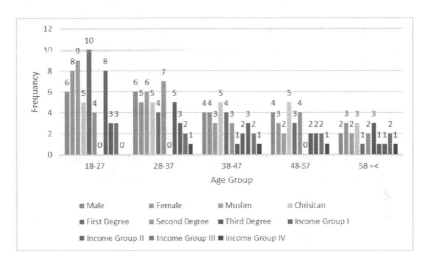

Of the total of 12 informants who said they have a very good passion (4) for digital trading, the female to male proportion was equally 6 (50%), while we have 4 (33.33%) Muslims and 8 (66.66%) Christians. What is more, 4 (33.33%) of them have a first degree, while 6 (50%), and 2 (16.66%) of them have second and third degrees, respectively. Likewise, we have 3 (25%) informants from the first- and second-income group, while 4 (33.33%) and 2 (16.66%) from the last two consecutive income groups, congruently.

Coming to the informants who said they have the best passion ever (5) for digital trading, we have 17 (51.51%) females and 16 (48.48%) males. On the other hand, there are 18 (54.54%) Muslims and 15 (45.45%) Christians. What is more, 18 (54.54%), 14 (42.42%), and I (3.03%) people have first, second and third degrees, compatibly. By the same token, we have 15 (45.45%), 9, (27.22%) 7 (21.21%), and 2 (6.06%) informants falling in one to four income groups in a raw.

In conclusion, there are a total of 23 (51.51%) females and 22 (48.88%) males having either a very good or best passion for digital trading. Likewise, we have 26 (57.77%) Muslims and 19 (42.22%) Christians. Moreover, there are 22 (44.44%), 20 (42.22%), and 3 (6.66%) first-degree to third-degree holders, disparately. Last, we have 18 (40%), 12 (26.66%), 11 (24.24%), and 4(8.88%) informants from one to four income categories in a raw.

From the above discussion, one can observe the fact the female to male proportion seems to be at balance with one or two percent difference, which might signify the passion of both genders to digital trading finds itself almost at the same bandwidth while Muslims are more passionate than Christians.

When it comes to the academic degree, most of them are first- and second-degree holders, which could highlight as people attain the third degree, they don't tend to do business online. In terms of income, a high concentration of passion is seen on people in the first two income groups as compared to the last two clutches, which slightly exhibits the deterioration of the public passion for digital marketing as income raises. Equally, as age increases passion seems to go down, which might suggest the younger the generation is more passionate we could get to digital trading.

Be that as it may, before finalizing the above finding in this regard, we must make sure whether the answers are statistically significant. To this end, a chi-square test was conducted to emphasize and accept the answer and support the above-inferred assumption. The null hypothesis (H0) assumes that public passion for digital trading at kickoff time is poor (1) and very poor (2), or below average/good (3), while the non-null hypothesis assumes very good (4) and best (5).

Figure 17. Public Passion at Kickoff: Chi-square Test

χ^2 Goodness of Fit

χ^2	df	p
9.80	1	0.002

As shown in the above table the chi-square as a test of independence whether or not to accept or reject a null hypothesis, is calculated by JAMOVIA and goes to be 0.002. Thus, the degree of significance is well below the accepted standard of 0.005. Hence, the null hypothesis is rejected, in this regard. In other words, the answers are not due to the chance and/or absence of a possible sampling error.

To put it otherwise, there is no significant deviation between the alleged and expected data when the curve of the observed frequencies is super-imposed on the curve of expected frequencies. Hence, the non-null hypothesis is accepted, and the finding is valid.

4.2.2. Public Passion After Experiencing a Recurrent Internet Outage

Internet access has been declared plainly as a basic human right by the UN back in 2011. This has not stopped countries like Ethiopia from routinely interrupting Internet access to their citizens (Itimu, 2019). Miscellaneous data exhibit that connectivity with the country's only internet provider, state-run Ethiopia Telecom, which expedites the process of deactivating national internet and telephony services, has been providing the Ethiopian authorities an effective internet cut off whenever required to repress public political instabilities originating from the ethnic-based political creed (Internet cut in Ethiopia amid unrest following the killing of singer, 2020).

Hence, there have been several nationwide internet blackouts, leaving friends and families disconnected, online businesses unable to operate, and journalists prevented from reporting on events (Woodhams, 2019). Thus, the internet users in Ethiopia have been complaining for a long that they could not access websites, messaging services such as Viber, WhatsApp, Telegram, and the likes. For instance, a global network of human rights organizations that work to end internet shutdowns has recently denounced the arbitrary use of internet shutdowns by the Government of Ethiopia in response to protests and unrest in the country (The Ethiopian government must end internet shutdowns to quell protests, 2020).

The outage has always been deliberate, obvious, and so alarming that it has almost reached a very shocking point of frustrating citizens who fully or partly depend on online services for information and/or conducting business (Fidelis, 2019). According to the NetBlocks, which determines the Internet performance and service reachability, official report, the loss of Ethiopia on Internet outage is estimated to be at least $4.5m every single day (Total internet outage identified in Ethiopia, 2019). NetBlocks maps the entire IP address space of the country in real-time to exhibit internet outages corresponding to Internet cuts in the region.

Often, such interruptions have a nation-scale impact affecting cellular and fixed-line networks. What is more, some report indicates that most of the Internet outages are not connected to any known international connectivity issues or any other technical outages (Ethiopia: Communications Shutdown Takes Heavy Toll, 2020). Habitually, Internet outage is done by the Ethiopian government to repress public demonstration against the rule (Solomon, As Violence Flares in Ethiopia, Internet Goes Dark, 2017).

These disruptions have widespread impacts on people and the economy with even partial disturbances affecting productivity, souring business confidence, and leading to lost opportunities (The economic impact of disruptions to Internet connectivity, 2016). One of these impacts falls on the public passion for digital trading. This part of the paper unveils the impact of the said outage on the passion of Ethiopians wanting to do business online.

To this end, the informants have been asked if they have encountered a sort of frequent outages. All of them, unanimously alleged that they have come across the outage multiple times. According to them, the great majority of these outages were made on purpose by the government to curb public resistance against the rule caused by the ethnic base politics imposed on them. This answer has been reinforced both in the focused group discussions and the interviews made at various times with some selected informants.

When asked if the outage has any significant impact on their respective passion for digital marketing, all in one accord said it does. Nevertheless, the level of the impact is not even across the board. Some have felt it so strong, while still were some who chanced to bear with it. To find out this difference, informants were asked to mark the degree of their respective public passion for digital marketing 1-5, 5 being best passion and 1 the lowest after the impact has been sensed. This question presupposes an identical null hypothesis (H0) and non-null hypothesis (H1) as discussed in the previous sub-topic. The subsequent table elucidates the chi-square test result highlighting the degree of significance.

Figure 18. Public Passion After Internet Outages: Chi-square Test

χ^2 Tests

	Value	df	p
χ^2	32.7	2	< .001
N	45		

As per the above test of independence made on JAMOVIA, there is a significant association between internet outages and the public passion for digital marketing, X2 (2, N = 45) = 32.5, p < .001. To exhibit the influence in a more demarcated and pictographic manner, a line graph is made underneath. The blue and the golden lines in the line graph denote public passion before and after the internet outage encounter, in turn. The red dots, on the other hand, entitles the tendency of the degeneration of the public passion as the internet outage persists.

Figure 19. Comparing Public Passion after Frequent Internet Outages

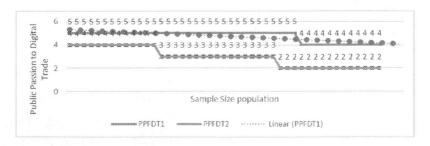

Comparing these results, at the kickoff stage where there was no frequent internet outage encountered, the number of informants who said their level of passion is the best or 5 out of 5, was 33 (73.33%) while there is no single informant who has a similar level of passion after the encounter. Instead, 13 (39 39%), 17 (51.51%), and 3 (9.09%) of them have gone one to three steps down in a raw.

On the other hand, at the kickoff stage, we have 12 (26.66%) informants who said they have a very good (4) passion for digital marketing. However, after the frequent outage encounter, all of them have dropped two steps down to poor passion (2).

Figure 20. Public Passion Before and After Internet Outages: Descriptive Test

Descriptive

	N	Mean	Median	SD	SE
PPFDT1	45	4.73	5	0.447	0.0667
PPFDT2	45	2.96	3	0.76	0.1187

In the above table, PPFDT1 and PPFDT1 indicate the public passion for digital marketing before and after an internet outage has been encountered. In the former case, the mean is 4.73 which is very much close to the 5, the best passion while the standard deviation is 0.447 which indicates the distribution of the data from the center. This might illustrate the central tendency of public passion to digital marketing, which divulges the fact that the informants have a passion very much closer to the best passion (5).

On the other hand, after the outage situation, we have a mean of 3 with a standard devotion of 0.796, which proves the central tendency is two steps away from the best passion (5). The variance between the before and after outage designates the impact which confirmations the decline of public passion approximately by an average value of 2.

4.2.3. Public Passion after Intimidation and Coercion

Some governments around the world engage in Internet surveillance (What Is Internet Surveillance and How to Avoid It, 2020). However, to protect the privacy of users and their other civil rights, they have put in place at least some sort of judicial and legislative devices. In Ethiopia, there is not enough attention made by concerned parties to put such a legislative device in place. Instead, the actual control by the government has been highly intensified as the scrupulous state-controlled internet surveillance is all over since EPRDF/PP has come to the office in the 1990th.

Monitoring of online transactions can justly be used to control illicit activities. Nonetheless, according to some reports, there is a lack or absence of rules and proper guidelines on internet scrutiny of communications or the use of collected information to ensure such practices are not illegitimate. This results in wide self-censorship, with many Ethiopians refraining from amenably doing business online and communicating on a multiplicity of topics across the telecom network (Telecom and Internet Surveillance in Ethiopia, 2014).

The Ethiopian government has been using full control of its telecom system and NISS as an instrument to crack down on online accounts of online businessmen, political dissenters, and other critics of the ruling party and to silence their dissenting voices and smash their trades (Ganesan, 2014). The Ethiopian security officials, by cracking down accounts, who seem to have virtually unlimited access to a third-party internet account, have been harassing internet users by verbally ordaining them to refrain and abstain from using the internet for some political reason.

In this regard, all the informants have agreed on the fact that there is this sort of intimidation by security officials against internet users. The issue has been brought to the focused group discussion and in the interview conducted with the selected informant for clarity's sake. In both instances, the issue of intimidation has been reported as a very exasperating episode.

To find out the impact of the intimidation, the informants were asked to mark the degree of their respective public passion for digital marketing 1-5, 5 being best passion and 1 the lowest assuming they have been intimidated by government security officials. The null hypothesis (H0) and non-null hypothesis (H1) are assumed to be very poor passion (1) and/or poor passion (2) and very good passion (4) and/or best of passion (5). The chi-square result below explains the degree of significance.

Figure 21. Public Passion Before and After Intimidation: Chi-square Test

χ^2 Tests

	Value	df	p
χ^2	36.2	2	< .001
N	45		

The chi-square test of independence above which was performed to examine the relationship between public passion for digital marketing and Intimidation and coercion. The relation between these variables is significant, X2 (1, N = 45) = 36.2, p = .001. Intimidation and coercion which keeps coming from the security officials can severely impact public passion for digital marketing. The succeeding linear graph offers the details of the impact.

Figure 22. Public Passion Before and After Intimidation: Chi-square Test

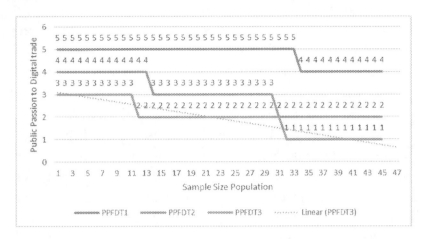

The blue line in the above linear graph shows public passion for digital marketing before both the internet outage is encountered and Intimidation and coercion have been made following the surveillance of the accounts of the informants. The golden and the gray lines, on the other hand, represent the public passion for digital marketing after both the internet outage and Intimidation and coercion have been encountered. The blue dots, on the other hand, presents the trend of the decline of the public passion for digital marketing.

Comparing the result with the kickoff stage, 33 (73.33%) and 12 (26.66%) informants having best of passion (5) and very good passion (4) while 11 (24.44%) of them have dropped two steps down to average passion (3), 20 (44.44%) of them dropped two steps down to very poor passion (2), and 2 (4.44%) dropped three solid steps down to very poor passion (1), while all of the informants who leveled themselves having a very good passion to digital marketing at the kickoff stage have dropped three steps to very poor passion (1).

Figure 23. Public Passion Before and After Intimidation: Descriptive Test

Descriptive

	N	Mean	Median	SD	SE
PPFDT1	45	4.73	5	0.447	0.0667
PPFDT3	45	1.93	2	0.751	0.1119

PPFDT1 and PPFDT3 represent the public passion for digital marketing at the kickoff stage and after intimidation and coercion have been experienced by the informants, in turn. The median and the mean for the first situation are 5 and 4.73 while for the second situation it is 2 and 1.93. In the first instance, the central tendency is between 4 and 5.

The lowest passion observed in this scenario is 4.283 which is well above the very good passion (4) level. However, in the second instance, the central tendency drops between 1 and 2, to be more precise, it is 1.07 which is very close to the poor (1). The difference between the two is 3.217.

This is a gigantic variance that prominences the adverse impact of intimidation and coercion on the public passion for digital marketing. The people involved with digital marketing seem to withdraw or drop off interest in a significant manner. This, in the long run, will not only have a hostile consequence on the growth of the economy of the country, but it could also lead to a sort of digital divide by relegating and obstructing the advancement of digital marketing.

4.2.4. Conclusion: Impact of Tribal Politics on Public Passion to Digital Marketing

The 21st century has introduced the key changes and developments in ICT. On the other hand, the contribution of the expansion of ICT to the development of digital trade has been enormous. Today, it has been reached a point where economic growth and social changes are almost inevitable given the digital world is out of the scene. In other words, the digital milieu has helped make things better and easier for society to do business online, and to do it fast and best with ease of doing things at a click.

It has to be noted that most of this growth in absolute values has been accounted for by the high-income economies. The developing economies such as Ethiopia have been severely stressed out by the ethnic-based political ideology that has been running the country for about three decades. Public passion for doing business online has been severely impacted.

As seen in the study, at the kickoff stage, public passion has been observed very high with a mean of 4.73 and a standard deviation of 0.447 along with a degree of significance of 0.001. Nevertheless, with the assumption of a frequent internet outage, which is deliberately made to surpass public upheavals against the rule, the mean has come down to 2.95 with a standard deviation of 0.796 bust same degrees of significance as the above.

This is a considerably visible change. There is a detectible difference between the central tendency of the public passion for digital marketing in the above-mentioned two scenarios. To be more precise, the difference is 1.78 which is enormous to observe and mark the impact of internet outages on the public passion for digital marketing.

With the notion that intimidation and coercion have been carried out, the mean and the standard deviation got to ne 1.93 and 0.751, respectively. Intimidation and coercion get hardened after the unauthorized surveillance made against internet users by the government security officials who break into the user's account illegally without a court warranty at hand.

As these evil measures of coercion get tightened, the impact of racially built politics on the public passion for digital marketing has essentially got augmented and increase. For instance, the difference between the first and third means has grown to 2.942, even worsening the assumed impact.

In conclusion, public passion for digital marketing and ethnic-based triable political ideology has a significant association. Given all the ingredients of digital trading being favorable and at a good stand, just when the degree of the practice and manifestation of the ethnic-based triable political ideology increases the public passion for digital marketing gets relentlessly impacted.

This is so because, as observed in Ethiopia, ethnic-based triable political ideology manufactures such elements as severe corruption, bad governance, unfairness, lack of democracy, and rule of law. Hence, such aftermaths as mass killing, and displacement would take place in many folds. This in turn would lead to public political upheavals, impatience, and instability.

To control such upheavals, the government has been observed taking measures as internet shutdown, security surveillance of private internet accounts by government security apparatus, leading to spying individuals, and harassing them from behind to the point of pressing false allegations and charges against them. Putting all together, this has viciously impacted public passion for digital marketing, which in turn might lead to a digital divide given the political setting remains the same.

4.3. The Prospect of Digital Divide in Ethiopia

A digital divide is any irregular dispersal in the access to, use of, or impact of ICT between any number of diverse groups, which can be defined based on social, geographical, or geopolitical criteria, or otherwise (Pillow, 2020). The digital divide can transpire within a given country or among counties across the board (BOURGEOIS, 2019). It can take place within any given nation, developed or developing, regardless, between the rich, educated, and powerful, and those who are not.

Though it is less often noted, the digital divide can also occur following linguistic and cultural gaps between people within a nation or otherwise. To mention but few, in the United States, where well over 95% of all inhabitants speak fluent English, there are differences in access to ICTs among different ethnic and cultural groups (Keniston, 2003). This paper, however, is very much concerned with a digital divide that may occur between the rich and the poor nations with a special focus on Ethiopia and the rest of the world.

The 1999 United Nations Report on Human Development devotes much of a chapter to the widening gap between the information-rich nations of the North and the information-poor nations of the South. At one extreme are the United States and the 'Nordic' countries like Sweden, Germany, Finland, and Iceland, where household telephone connectivity is well over 90%, computer saturation is over 50%, and home-based Internet connectivity averages over 50%.

At the other extreme lies most of Africa, most of South America, South Asia, China, Indonesia, and so on -- the 80% of the world where telephone connectivity is 3% or less (less than 30 million/1 billion in India), home computer ownership is 1 - 2% and Internet connectivity less than half of that.

The reason why the digital divide between nations is cumulatively swelling seems clear. If any given country gives extensive access to ICT to its citizens, it gives the nation an advantage to develop quicker more profoundly, and thoughtfully, and the absence of access might leave it on the verge of a disadvantage.

This might have everything to do with the amount of attention the country has offered to the expansion of ICT. In a country like Ethiopia, ICT does not seem to get due consideration from the ruling party for various reasons, all emanating from the racial constructed identity politics lashing the nation for the last three solid decades.

A question was asked to get hold of the thoughts of the informants on whether or not the digital divide would be a perspective threat to Ethiopia given the tribal politics would remain in force as much as it has been thus far. As seen below in the output of the JAMOVIA form one-sample chi-square test of a single population, the Observed response for "Yes" is 29 (64.4%) while for "No" and "Not Sure" were, 11 (24.4%) and 5 (11.1%), respectively.

The Expected return of each one of the categories was 15. What is more, asymptotic significance is displayed. The significance level is 0.001. A focused group discussion was held about make sure if the answers were given with a proper understanding of the intent in them. Both, these discussions, and the interview held to further verify if the return yielded alien to what they mean, confirm the fact that the informs answered the questions about the digital divide with a proper understanding of what it is and how it can impact the growth of the country.

Figure 24. Public Passion Before and After Intimidation: Chi-square Test

χ^2 Goodness of Fit

χ^2	df	p
20.8	2	< .001

The value of the chi-square is 20.8. The probability of getting that chi-square if the null hypothesis was true is 0. This underlines the fact that the data collected for this research is well far from incidental happening. Therefore, the null hypothesis is rejected, and by so doing, the probability of the occurrence of the digital divide seems to be likely.

Figure 25. Public Passion Before and After Intimidation: Binomial Test

						95% Confidence Interval	
	Level	Count	Total	Proportion	p	Lower	Upper
ProbDD	1	29	45	0.644	0.072	78	.781
	2	11	45	0.244	<.001	0.1288	0.395
	3	5	45	0.111	<.001	0.0371	0.241

Note. H_a is proportion $\neq 0.5$

As shown in the above binomial test the probability for "No" and "Not Sure" answers to occur is less than 0.1%, which signifies they are unlikely to happen. On the contrary, the "Yes" answer has a 7.2% probability to happen. In other words, the test confirms the fact that 29 (64.44%) of the informants think chances are digital divide would happen with a probability of about 7.2% to transpire.

4.3.1. Conclusion: The Prospect of Digital Divide in Ethiopia

Being a country with a population of about 115 million people with an expected growth of that would exceed 200 million by the end of 2049 running at the rate of 2.7% annually with no projected peak year, Ethiopia is hoped to be the next big emerging market in Africa (Worldmeters, 2019). There are quite a few details of reasons for the assessment.

First, Ethiopia is home to some of the youngest populations in the world having over 70% of its population under 25 years of age (Burton, 2017). Second, Ethiopia, as a country of the younger generation in the world, promises to be a major consumption market over the next three decades. Third, Ethiopia has quite a significant number of its people, according to some reports up to 30%, in school, working towards meeting the need of the swinging educated workforce around the world.

Regardless of these details, the potential remains exasperated, mainly because of the ethnically constructed hostile political decree underway in the country. According to the findings of this research, unless otherwise, the government reverses the gears of its politics to include all impartially honoring the rights of the individual as a citizen while equally acknowledging and respecting all other rights, for the digital divide to occur with a 7.8% of probability is a matter of time.

4.4. Country Level Political Risk in Ethiopia

The impact of identity-based politics in Ethiopia is not limited only to affecting the passion of citizens to digital marketing. It also affects investment in the arena coming from both local and international investors[29]. It goes without saying that when the instability in the country increases investment would decrease[30]. There are more than adequate indicators demonstrating a country-level political risk in Ethiopia arising from the rude practice of identity politics. Before further debate on the subject,

[29] Solomon Gizaw (January 10, 2020), Identity Politics and Its Impact on Public Passion for Digital Marketing, Interview by Daniel Solomon
[30] Sara Solomon (January 12, 2020), Identity Politics and Its Impact on Public Passion for Digital Marketing, Interview by Daniel Solomon

it is important to clearly define what a country-level Political risk is and how it matters in Ethiopia's current situation.

A country-level political risk usually represents the risk that economic, social, and political conditions where local or international incidents or a combination of the two would affect investment in a country (Toksöz, 2014). It refers to the broader notion of the degree to which political and economic turmoil impinge on the securities of issuers doing business in a particular country (Bouchet, 2018). In this regard, these issuers could be local or foreign investors or any other sources that might want to spend in the country in one or another way.

All said country-level political risk refers to the risk of investing in a country, dependent on changes in the business environment that may adversely affect operating profits or the value of assets in a specific country (Daniel, 2012). Stability factors such as mass riots, civil war, and other potential events contribute to the operational risks. In short, country risk is a more general term that generally refers only to risks affecting all investors operating within a particular country. To manage country risk, the concerned bodies should identify, measure, and monitor risks and control their level of exposure to it.

4.4.1. Some Indicators of a Country Level Risk in Ethiopia

Given the discussion thus far, the passion for digital marketing seems to be severely impacted by various factors emerging from the identity politics that the country has been pursuing for the last three decades. Below are some of the most outlying indicators ever observed signifying the inevitability of a country-level risk in the country.

a. The continuation of the constitution which legitimizes identity-based politics,
b. Unceasing political instability,
c. Mass killings based on ethnic profile and religious background,
d. Incessant conflict and fighting between regional states and/or the government and some regional states such as Tigray,
e. Bad political narratives that demonstrate a certain ethnic group as an oppressor against others
f. Corruption, hypnotism, bad governance, and lack of law and order.

The above indicators are ready in place in the country. The Constitution that declares the country as a coming together nation is still in power supporting the various nations and nationalities as autonomous states and the different political parties to be established based on such ethnic profiles. This in turn has led the country into a series of political instability, mass killings, ethnic cleansing, incessant conflict, and fighting between regional states and/or the government and some regional states such as Tigray,

Putting together, Ethiopia would have much more county-level risks than any other nation in the world that has political stability along with internet penetration and technological advancement. When the country-level risk arguments, investors demand higher returns as compensation for this added risk or they will step back. This, in turn, causes lesser investment in technological advancement, be it by the government and/or private investors, which hinders the progress of digital marketing and by so doing facilitates the occurrence of the digital divide in the country.

4.4.2. Country Level Risk Management Framework

The political environment in a country can have a major bearing on its risk exposure. It is the duty and responsibility of the government to identify, manage and control risks across your entire nation. There are quite a several risk managements tools and frameworks available out there. Among them, ERM (Enterprise Risk Management), ORM (Operational Risk Management), Governance, Risk, and Compliance (GRC), and IRM (Integrated Risk Management) are the most popular ones (Miller, 1992). MLMG (Machine Learning Model Governance) is also another tool that can be used to mitigate risks at a large scale.

All of them support comprehending the risk exposure of a given entity and to curve the risks and then take on new opportunities permitting expansion and development based on the measured analysis. They can facilitate, connect, and measure risks across the entity so that potential risk management strategies would be taken care of beforehand (Daniel, 2012). These risks could occur at a small or large scale to the point they can destroy investment ventures in a country if they are not well taken care of in an appropriate manner[31].

However, to help manage and reverse the political risks that contemporary Ethiopia has encountered, IPRMF (Integrate Political Risk Management Framework) framework is customized for a couple of reasons. First, most of the available frameworks are much about risks associated with companies and organizations at the enterprise level. They do not deal with matters on issues affecting investment at a country level.

---

[31] Cyrus Hailu (Septiembre 06, 2019), Online Customers Market Preference, Interview by Daniel Solomon

Second, though, some of them take instability into account, they do not give due attention to a kind of political unrest emanating from identity-based poetics. As a sort of comprehensive risk management information system, most of them do not serve for identifying, reducing, and financing risk across all lines of situations. Most of all, they are not primarily meant to address risks after they have already occurred. Therefore, their applicability is minimal or insignificant to help mitigating political risks in a country like Ethiopia which has already been affecting the nation for years now.

4.5. IPRMF (Integrate Political Risk Management Framework)

A county exists to protect and create benefits for its citizens, and the vision and the mission statements along with the core values and the strategies of the Political parties that govern the country define the scope and extent of those benefits. However, these statements alone cannot protect the rights of the citizens and create the desired fruits of benefits, and many countries use political parties as the change vehicle to deliver the capability which leads to the required benefits. In some cases, these parties come to office thru election, while others by armed struggle like the case are for EPRDF.

The political ideology these parties matter the most in protecting the rights of citizens and help them get the desired benefits as citizens. Unfortunately, the identity-based partisan philosophy that EPRDF came up with did not seem to work for Ethiopia. It has already caused several damages to the unity and stability of the country.[32]. Citizens have been divided according

---

[32] Solomon Gizaw (January 10, 2020), Identity Politics and Its Impact on Public Passion for Digital Marketing, Interview by Daniel Solomon

to their ethnic profile and were fed quite a horrible narration of hatred which caused mass killings, ethnic cleansing, political upheavals, and unrest[33].

This, in turn, has severely impacted the technological advancement of the country along with the passion of its people for digital marketing. As sown in the findings of this research if due measures are not taken by concerned authorities to get rid of identity politics the country has over 7% probability to fall into digital divided soon. Hence, to manage and reverse the country-level political risk that the country has already encountered IPRMF is custom designed as a solution framework.

IPRMF is a political risk management framework that would help countries whose political ideology is obstructing investment in one or another way. It is integrated simply because it takes a holistic approach to address the issue from the ground up. It is much about understanding the big picture of the problem by going into its root causes and trying to address it from a nationwide level.

4.5.1. IPRMF Tenets

IPRMF strictly adheres to the following four tenets:

a. Functional fluidity: IPRMF investigates the risk from multiple angles and directions. It has functional fluidity and positional flexibility. It is not rigged and finger-pointing. What is more, it is not to blame a certain entity. Instead, it focuses on understanding the root cause of the problem and addresses it in such a way that it never impacts anymore.

---

[33] Cyrus Hailu (Septiembre 06, 2019), Online Customers Market Preference, Interview by Daniel Solomon

b. Evidence-based research: IPRMF gives due credit to research-based evidence. Every single issue must be well researched, analyzed, and synthesized. The research must be evidence-based which is true to the ground.

c. Relevant skillsets: Most relevant, experienced, and pertinent skillsets must participate in IPRMF. It goes by merit not by other means and ways.

d. Defined slandered and principles: IPRMF is dedicated to defined standards and principles as well. The team to be involved in IPRMF must set a sort of guidelines, directions, principles, and redlines that must be strictly followed.

4.5.2. IPRMF Process Steps

IPRMF is a process tool that contains the subsequent five important steps:

a. Preliminary stage: This stage includes but is not limited to establishing the IPRMF team, preparing the necessary principles, guidelines, rules, and commitment levels. The palming, budgeting, setting procedures, and identifying deliverables along, delivery schedules, scopes, and possible limitations, and mitigation strategies might also be included in this period.

b. Investigative stage: In this stage, the IPRMF team would start collecting both primary and secondary sources that would help to understand the causes of the poetical risk. The resources could be collected through reviewing pertinent literature, questionnaire, focused group discussions, and interview with appropriate individuals and concerned governmental bodies. The collection must be as exhaustive as possible.

c. Analysis and recommendation: At this stage, the IPRMF team must work on the data it has accumulated. This work includes verifying the candidacy of the data, analyzing it using scientific methods, discussing the finding with concerned parties for further improvement, and finally binding the outcome with a meaningful user guide.

d. Implementation and maintenance: At this stage, the IPRMF team in collaboration with all concerned parties and stakeholders, will start implementing the outcome of its findings and recommendations safely. This may include public discussion, amendments of rules and constitutions, restructuring the structure of the government, declaring new laws and orders, etc.

The entire process of IPRMF implements the agile-scrum methodology, where the citizens would be considered as customers, while their representatives act as product owners. The rest of the crew will act as developers (who develops the solution), testers (who verifies if the solution works), a business analyst who works with the customer to find out what works the best for them, the scrum master, and the project manager as assigned by the due office.

Then, the key epics will be gathered and placed as the product backlog, where the user stories, technical stories and enable stories will be made during the sprint planning session by the team. IPRMF team will have product grooming, sprint planning, a stand-up meeting, and a retroactive meeting.

In the product grooming meeting, items that will be dealt with in the fourth coming sprint will be selected, while in the sprint planning work items will be distributed among the team. In the everyday stand-up meeting, each member of the team will present what s/he has accomplished yesterday, what s/he will accomplish today, and if s/he has faced any impediment.

The scrum master will take notes of the meeting and if there is any impediment observed, s/he would help to address it within a couple of days. If the impediment still pertains and is not addressed, the scrum master will communicate to the president of the team, and all other concerned stakeholders so that the issue could be leveled as a work stoppage, and all be seriously involved to address it. Every two weeks, a sprint panning would take place followed by a retroactive meeting where the team states what went well in the last sprint, what went unsatisfactory, and the lessons learned from the entire process.

Using agile as its methodology IPRMF delivers incrementally on two weeks basis. It does start from the most significant one and bit by bit and in a small chunk, it keeps delivering the product which is the solution that will remove the risk. Therefore, IPRMF is a sort of iterative model that keeps producing deliverables until the risk is eliminated.

Chapter Five

CONCLUSION AND RECOMMENDATION

THE SWIFT DEVELOPMENT OF ICT has provided new opportunities for individuals to communicate and do online businesses in a manner and at a pace like never, aggregating the space for digital marketing and expediting access to information. It is extensively used across various industries, from marketing and telecom to education. Consequently, the global ICT expenditure is expected to surge to over $6 trillion by 2022 (Picincu, 2018).

In short, ICT has become an increasingly important tool for development, providing access to information for science, technology, and innovation, expediting ease of doing online business and digital marketing, nurturing, and improving local, regional, and international cooperation and knowledge-sharing. This chapter presents the conclusion and the recommendations of the research work.

5.1. Conclusion

Developed nations worldwide are making the best out of ICT. They continue to leverage all of their good returns to increase productivity in the workplace, cut operational costs and improve their national economy, and advance the life experience of their respective citizens (Dillinger, 2017). On the contrary, many developing nations seem not to be able to enjoy these opportunities for various reasons. Ethiopia is one of these countries coming in the frontline.

Among many other actions such as sabotage, corruption, less attention, and poor budgeting to the development of ICT, by shutting the internet, scrutineering, and intimidating internet users, the abettors of the ethnic-based political ideology seem to have a severe impact on the growth and expansion of digital marketing in the country.

Internet shutdowns and disruptions are sometimes applied to specific services like social media, instant messaging, or search rather than the whole Internet ecosystem. Blocking these services which people and businesses use daily has immediate impacts. Such disturbances make it even more challenging for people to connect, discover products online, and obtain information from the web. This makes businesses lose visibility with customers, and opportunities to interact with them, obtain feedback and receive orders. In short, it hampers the growth of digital marketing to its fullest scope.

On top of that, to spy the use private internet users and have control over the type of information they access and manipulate, be it business, politics, social, or otherwise, the government has maintained a strong hold of the Internet. Therefore, internet users including those who do digital marketing on the web encounter harassment and threat by the security apparatus of the rule.

As it has been discovered in the focused discussions and interviews conducted for this study, the informants have witnessed some Ethiopians who have been told to quit their online activities or else they would be incarcerated. Some more citizens have been jailed, tortured, and even sued for their active involvement on the internet. Still were some more who have been embattled with highly cutting-edge surveillance tools designed to clandestinely monitor online activity and rip-off passphrases and personal documents without court warrants.

There is a piece of strong evidence that attests and confirms the association of public passion to digital marketing and the impact of ethnic-based politics. As indicated in the hypothetical part of the research where a sort of theoretical framework is molded, public passion for digital marketing and the impact of ethnic-based politics seem to be inversely proportional. When the pressure that coils from such a political setting gets intensified in the form of internet blockage and intimidation of internet users by breaking into their private accounts to know what they are up to and take action against them, public passion gets significantly deteriorated.

The root cause of the political pressure, on the other hand, is the ethnic-based politics that has reformed and reconstructed the country according to the racial profiles of its citizens. Following such politics, various ethnic groups were trained to develop abhorrence against Amhara ethnic group and the Amharic language.

Hence, they started to push back against mainly against Amhara. Subsequently, violence and wildness get escalated at times one against the other ethnic group, and at other times against the regime. In this regard, thousands of civilians have been displaced, tones of properties have been turned to ash, thousands more have been jailed and even killed.

The influence made by the internet most importantly social media and messaging tools such as Facebook, Twitter, Instagram, WhatsApp, Viber, and the likes had been tremendous to the point that the government started to investigate it as a potential platform that catalyzes the mess around.

Therefore, internet blockage and shutdown along with spying and intimidating some selected groups became daily routines of the government whenever political upheavals and mayhems get manifested, which in turn has impacted the ease of doing digital marketing under question. Apart from the impact on fundamental rights, some report indicates that internet shutdown in Ethiopia each day caused a loss more than $4.5 million (Internet shutdown costs Ethiopia $100 million, 2020).

In conclusion, as long such identity-based politics is put to stop, ceased, and/or improved into something appealing on the idea, social values, and principles, digital marketing will continue to upset. Besides, the more digital marketing is hurt, the more the probable coincidental chance is for the digital divide to transpire and become apparent. In other words, given things would go as is in the political arena of the country without a major change to the political framework that has its foundation on ethnic federalism, the prospect of the occurrence of the digital trade in Ethiopia might hit a probability up to 7.8%.

Getting out of this divide might be very expensive and hard to comprehend and materialize. Therefore, the researcher cannot emphasize enough the following recommendation to various stakeholders to curve the danger before it is too late to reverse it.

5.2. Recommendation to the Ethiopian Government

a. Use the framework suggested in this research and to look into its political structure and philosophy, and the repercussion therefrom, and identify concerns, issues, enigmas impeding the advance of digital technology within the nation and among its citizens and reverse them,

b. Put a legal and binding embargo for all political parties founded or yet to be found, not to be instituted on identity, religion, social creed, rituals, and traditional practice, and if they already are, streamline themselves based on the political idea within a stipulated period and if otherwise disband them from the political prospect.

c. Revisit and review the Constitution of The Federal Democratic Republic of Ethiopia and with the full consent of the citizens amend and rewrite those articles that provide a legal and circumstantial context to the ethnic federalism of the country.

d. Replace or restructure the constitutions of the ethnic federal assembly and rebuild the nation in such a manner that citizens live at equal footing with equal privileges and according to their respective skill, profession, and contribution in the workforce.

e. Encourage and embolden the development and expansion of the ICT sector by investing enough and letting the private sector capitalize and contribute in the field as much by systematizing, modernizing, and digitalizing the country.

f. Impose the necessity of a court warrant before interception and surveillance of private documents and archives.

g. Discontinue manipulating the internet for political causes such as internet blockage to arrest public upheavals, spying and harassing individuals for exercising their rights out there on the internet and elsewhere on the ground.

5.3. Recommendation to the People of Ethiopia be it Diaspora or Local

a. As the world is fast approaching to be a small village, in this epoch of technology, break your shell inside out and start to think outside the box of identity politics, honor and give due dignity to your fellow brother regardless of who he is and what he believes in, and work on yourself as one people and one country indivisible, under God.

b.   Given the swift technological advancement, never fail behind, instead take the lead in the pattern and feature of technological advancement including the digital ecosphere, get released from the ground and be online and get connected with the rest of the world, share your indigenous skills, and learn from others.

c.   Work joyfully and if need be, even digitally with all the earnest it takes to be effective by believing in yourself as somebody critically important to the development, peace, prosperity, and democracy of your contemporary world, and most importantly to your beloved country.

5.4. Recommendation to the External World: Governments and Organizations

a.   Develop strategies to mitigate the risk of trade unease, concentration and monopoly of technology and monetary power in the hands of very few countries, the hazard of the manifestation of a digital divide in countries such as Ethiopia by investing enough and working out its citizens, and all other misapplications and abuses allied to online businesses and digital marketing operations.

b.   Regulate the export and trade of surveillance and censorship technologies such as deep packet inspection equipment and intrusion software that compromise confidentiality and damage the privacy of internet users and by so doing obstruct the development and expansion of digital marketing.

c. Re-ruminate on human rights due to thoroughness on ICT related projects in Ethiopia, to prevent being ancillary to the violations of the rights to privacy or freedom of expression, association, or movement; or access to information including through censorship, illegal surveillance, or network shutdowns conducted by the government if any.

References

(2005)., O. f.-o. (2007, 12 15). Good practice paper on ICTs economic growth and poverty reduction. Retrieved from http://www.oecd. org/dataoecd/2/46/35284979.pdf

Abate, N. (2015). Ethiopia: Misuse of social media and the threat it imposes to our coexistence. Norway: ECADF.

Abawi, D. K. (2013). Data Collection Instruments. Geneva: Training in Sexual and Reproductive Health Research Committee.

Abdu, B. (2019, 04 19). Ethnic politics: the peril of Ethiopia? The Reporter.

Abelow, A. D. (2020, Jan). If Our Future Is Digital, How Will It Change the World? Retrieved from WIRED: https://www.wired.com/ insights/2014/04/future-digital-will-change-world/

Adamu, A. Y. (2019). Ethnic Violence Challenging Ethiopian Universities. The world view.

Ademo, M. (2012, 08 19). Media restrictions tighten in Ethiopia. CJR.

Aden, L. (2018, 04 30). Understanding what is happening in ICT in Ethiopia: A Supply- and Demand-side Analysis of the ICT Sector. Retrieved from African Portal: https://www.africaportal. org/publications/understanding-what-happening-ict-ethiopia- supply-and-demand-side-analysis-ict-sector/

Admin. (2019, 06 19). Internet shutdown has continued in Ethiopia. Retrieved from Ayaantu News: http://ayyaantuu.org/ internet-shutdown-has-continued-in-ethiopia/

Afrito. (2019). Ethiopia Travel Guide. Retrieved from Africa: https:// www.africatouroperators.org/ethiopia/ethiopia-travel-guide

Akl, A. (2014, Oct 2). Fear of 'New' Creates Digital Divide for Older Users. VOA.

Akrani, G. (2013). Limitations of Marketing Research - Demerits of MR.

Aldonas, U. A. (2015). Addressing Barriers to Digital Trade. E15 Expert Group.

Alexander, J. (2017). *Financial Planning & Analysis and Performance Management (Wiley Finance)* 1st *Edition*.

Ambaye, D. T. (2019, 06 19). *Ethiopia blocks internet for national exams - Net Blocks. African news*.

Araba Sey, C. R. (2013). *Connecting people for development: Why public access ICTs matter. Global Impact Study of Public Access to ICTs Final research report*.

Article Menu, J. D. (2018, 03 19). *Democratic Digital Inequalities: Threat and Opportunity in Online Citizenship From Motivation and Ability. American Behevariol Scientist*.

Aryal, S. (2019, 03 17). *Questionnaire method of data collection. Retrieved from https://microbenotes.com/questionnaire-method-of-data-collection/*

Asfaw, A. A. (2015, 11 1). *The Consequences of Ethnic Federalism in Ethiopia. ECADF*.

Assefa, M. (2019). *Role of social media in Ethiopia's recent political transition. Research Gate*.

Babatunde, M. (2016, 10 05). *The average value for Ethiopia during that period was -1.44 points with a minimum of -1.8 points in 2007 and a maximum of -0.63 points in 1998 (Bank, 2017). This shows that the country is not performing that well from 1996 to 2017 where digital trading w. Face Africa, p. 1*.

Bada, F. (2017, 09 07). *world atlas. Retrieved from Which Countries Are Part Of Central Africa?: https://www.worldatlas.com/articles/which-countries-are-part-of-central-africa.html*

Badwaza, Y. (2019). *Ethiopia has seen dramatic political changes this year, but significant challenges remain. The United States should seize this opportunity to support a genuine democratic transition in a pivotal country. Freedom House*.

Bahru, Z. (2018). *A History of Modern Ethiopia, 1855-1991. thrift books*.

Bala, M. (2020). *A Critical Review of Digital Marketing. SSRN*.

Beckwith, H. (2019). *Selling the Invisible: A Field Guide to Modern Marketing. New York: Amazon Books*.

Bedasso, G. G. (2018, 02 07). *Managing Ethiopia's political crisis. Opinion Africa.*

Belay, F. Y. (2016). *Conceptualizations and Impacts of Multiculturalism in the Ethiopian Education System. The University of Toronto.*

Belcastro, H. (2010, 01 01). *ICTs for Democracy: Information and Communication Technologies for the Enhancement of Democracy.* Retrieved from http://comminit.com/democracy-governance/content/icts-democracy-information-and-communication-technologies-enhancement-democracy

Bennett, N. J. (2017). *Bennett, N. J., Roth, R., Klain, S. C., Chan, K., Conservation social science: Understanding and integrating human dimensions to improve conservation. Bennett, N. J., Roth, R., Klain, S. C., Chan, K., Christie, P., Clark, D. A., ... Wyborn, C. (2017). Conservation sociaBiological Conservation.*

Berhe, M. g. (2016). *Laying the Past to Rest: The EPRDF and the Challenges of Ethiopian State: New.*

Betemariam, T. (2020, 09 28). *Current Political Situation of Ethiopia in terms of Promoting Digital Marketing. (D. Solomon, Interviewer)*

Bhalerao, P. K. (2010). *Sample size calculation. International Journal of Ayurveda Research, 1.*

Bhat, A. (2019, 10). *POPULATION DATA: DEFINITION, CLASSIFICATION, ESTIMATION, AND IMPORTANCE.* Retrieved from QuestionPro: https://www.questionpro.com/blog/population-data/

Blanke, J. (2016, 01 19). *Is technological change creating a new global economy?* Retrieved from World Economic Forum: https://www.weforum.org/agenda/2016/01/is-technological-change-creating-a-new-global-economy/

Bloor, M. F. (2001). *Focus groups in social research. Thousand Oaks, CA: Sage Publications Inc.*

Bodla, D. B. (2018). *Research Methodology.* Retrieved from Meaning of research: http://ddegjust.ac.in/studymaterial/mba/cp-206.pdf

Bongo, P. (2005). *The impact of ICT on economic growth.* Retrieved from http://129.3.20.41/eps/dev/papers/0501/0501008.pdf

Bordens, K. S. (1996). *Research design and methods: A process analysis* (3rd ed.). Mountain View.

Bouchet, M. H. (2018). *Managing Country Risk in an Age of Globalization: A Practical Guide to Overcoming Challenges in a Complex World* 1st ed.

BOURGEOIS, D. T. (2019). *Information Systems Beyond the Organization.*

Brown, N. E. (2020). *Distinct Identities (Routledge Series on Identity Politics)* 1st Edition. Amazon Books.

Burkitt-Gray, A. (2018). *'Virtual' competitors to be allowed to offer internet services in Ethiopia. Capacity.*

Burrows, D. &. (1997). *Focus groups: What are they and how can they be used in nursing and health care research? Social Sciences in Health.*

Burton, J. (2017). *30 Countries With The Youngest Populations In The World. World Atlas.*

C, K. (2012). *The New Threat of Digital Marketing. Pediatric Clinic.*

Calhoun, C. (1999). *Ethiopia's Ethnic Cleansing. Dissent.*

Cao, F. (2014). *Internet addiction among Chinese adolescents: prevalence and psychological features. Wiley Online Library.*

Carey, M. A. (1994). *Capturing the group effect in focus groups: A special concern in analysis. Qualitative Health Research.*

Carr, P. (2011, 01 09). *Technology and Developing Countries. Retrieved from University of Waterloo: https://impactofinformation systemsonsociety.wordpress.com/2011/01/09/week-2-technology-and-third-world-development/*

Cavallo, M. A. (2016, 12 21). *The growing importance of the technology economy. Retrieved from IDG Contributor Network: https://www.cio.com/article/3152568/the-growing-importance-of-the-technology-economy.html*

Cervellati, M. (2011). *Democratization, Violent Social Conflicts, and Growth. SSRN.*

Chan, S. (2016, 11 2016). *Digital Transformation and The Third Industrial Revolution. Linkedin.*

Chang, J. (2019). *A-List of Third World Countries: 10 Poorest Nations With Rising Economies*. Retrieved from FinancesOnline: https://financesonline.com/a-list-of-third-world-countries-10-poorest-nations-with-rising-economies/

Chanie, P. (2007). *Clientelism and Ethiopia's post-1991 decentralization*. The Journal of Modern African Studies., 45.

Chen, L. Z. (2019). *China's Digital Economy: Opportunities and Risks*. International Monetary Fund.

Chigozie, E. (2019). *AnswersAfrica*. Retrieved from East African Countries: List of Countries in East Africa: https://answersafrica.com/east-african-countries-list.html

Chinn, M. D. (2004). *The Determinants of the Global Digital: A Cross-Country Analysis of Computer and Internet Penetration*. Economic Growth Center.

Choudhrs, A. (2020). *Questionnaire Method of Data Collection: Advantages and Disadvantages*.

Cisler, S. (2001). *Subtract the digital divide*. Subtract the digital divide.

CJP. (2020). *CPJ condemns Ethiopian internet shutdown and Oromia Media Network raid*. CJP.

Conrow, E. H. (2017). *Effective Risk Management: Some Keys to Success*. Amazon Book Clubs.

Constitute. (2018, 01 18). Retrieved from Ethiopia's Constitution of 199: https://www.constituteproject.org/constitution/Ethiopia_1994.pdf

Corey, R. (2020). *Ethiopia's violent death toll rises to 239*. JP.

(2019). *Country comparison Ethiopia vs Kenya*. ountryeconomy.com.

Dahir, A. L. (2016). *Ethiopia's previously divided ethnic groups are unifying to protest against the government*. Quartz Africa.

Dahir, A. L. (2019, 06 18). *Ethiopia's tech startups are ready to run the world, but the internet keeps getting blocked*. Quartz Africa.

Daniel, W. (2012). *Managing Country Risk: A Practitioner's Guide to Effective Cross-Border Risk Analysis 1st Edition*.

David, C. (2009). *The Diffusion of the Internet a Cross-cultural Analysis*. Research Papers in Economics.

de Waal, A. (1997). Famine Crimes: Politics & the Disaster Relief Industry in Africa. Oxford: James Currey.

Dealatorre, K. C. (2019, 04 11). Democracy and the Digital Divide: Is Access Enough? Digital Impact.

Def. (2019). Digital Trade.

Deiss, R. (2018). Digital Marketing For Dummies, 2nd Edition. New York: Amazon Books.

Deloach, J. (2017). Managing Country Risk. Corporate Compliance Report.

Demissie, A. A. (2019). Sidama referendum: Over 98% vote 'YES' for Ethiopia's 10th regional state. African News.

Devaraj, S. S. (2017). Human Development & Technology in US Counties: Technology Quality & Accessibility Considerations for Policy Makers. Ball State University.

Dewan, S. (2018). The Digital Divide: Current and Future Research Directions1. The Paul Merage School of Business. Retrieved from https://pdfs.semanticscholar.org/d6c1/18d8c0461b350e9925103db435776714781d.pdf

Dewey, T. (2017). The Impact of Social Media on Social Unrest in the Arab Spring. Stanford University.

Diamond, S. (2018). Facebook Marketing. John Wiley a& Sons Inc.

Diaz, M. (2019). A Silent Majority: Internally Displaced People in Ethiopia. TASSC Advocacy.

Diffrent, M. (2017, 11 17). Ethiopia's internet crackdown hurts everyone. Retrieved from Ethiopian Today: https://ethiopian-today.blogspot.com/2016/11/ethiopias-internet-crackdown-hurts.html

(2019, 5 1). Digital Trade and U.S. Trade Policy. Congressional Research Service.

(2020). digital 2020: Ethiopia. Data Portal.

Dijk, J. v. (2018). A FRAMEWORK FOR DIGITAL DIVIDE. Journal of the University of Twente RESEARCH: The Pitfalls of a Metaphor.

Dillard, J. (2019). The Data Analysis Process: 5 Steps To Better Decision Making. Retrieved from BIG SKY: https://www.bigskyassociates.com/blog/bid/372186/The-Data-Analysis-Process-5-Steps-To-Better-Decision-Making

Dillinger, J. (2017). *Top Countries In The Information and Communication Technology Development Index. World Atlas.*

Economics, T. (2019, 06). *Ethiopia Interest Rate. Retrieved from Trading Economics: https://tradingeconomics.com/ethiopia/interest-rate*

Edewor, N. (2011). *Ethics and Social Issues Related to Information Communication Technology (ICT). Delta State Polytechnic, Nigeria.*

Elisa. (2008). *Information Society and Digital Divide. Polimetrica.*

El-Sherbiny, E. (2021). *Uganda, Ethiopia, Egypt... the hidden cost of internet blackouts. The African report.*

Elving, R. (2020). *Ethiopia Reflects On Its Founding Father's Triumphant, Bloody Legacy. NPR.*

Endeshaw, D. (2020). *Ethiopia passes a law imposing jail terms for internet posts that stir unrest. Returns.*

Engel, A. (2016). *Libya as a Failed State: Causes, Consequences, Options. The Washington Institute.*

ESAT. (2017, 11 8). *Ethiopia: Shortage of hard currency cripples the economy, says Governor of National Bank. Retrieved from ESAT NEWS: https://ethsat.com/2017/11/ethiopia-shortage-hard-currency-cripples-economy-says-governor-national-bank/*

Escsp. (2019). *INTERNATIONAL TRADE IN A DIGITAL AGE.*

Ethiopia. (2019). *Retrieved from Infopalace: https://www.infoplease.com/world/countries/ethiopia/prime-minister-meles-zenawi-dies*

(2018). *Ethiopia country profile. London: BBC.*

Ethiopia imposes a state of emergency as unrest intensifies. (2016, 10 16). *Retrieved from The Washington Post: https://www.washingtonpost.com/world/africa/ethiopia-imposes-state-of-emergency-as-unrest-intensifies/2016/10/10/7825391e-8ee9-11e6-bc00-1a9756d4111b_story.html?utm_term=.442655091d3e*

(2020). *Ethiopia Internet Users. Internet Live Stats.*

(2021). *Ethiopia Population Live. Worldometer.*

Ethiopia profile - Timeline. (2019, 06 06). *Retrieved from A chronology of key events: https://www.bbc.com/news/world-africa-13351397*

Ethiopia: Communications Shutdown Takes Heavy Toll. (2020). *Human Rights Watch.*

(2014). Ethiopia: General Information. Australia's Government Department of Foreign Affairs.

(2020). Ethiopia's internet penetration is less than half the African average. The Capital.

Ethiopia's ethnic conflicts destabilize Abiy's reforms. (2019, 11 01). Top Stories.

Evans, A. (2012, 08 19). Resource scarcity in Ethiopia. Retrieved from Global Dashboard: https://www.globaldashboard.org/2012/08/01/resource-scarcity-in-ethiopia/

(2021). Failed States. World Population Review.

Family Planning Program In Ethiopia Health And Social Care Essay. (2016). UKEssays.

Farrell, H. (2012). The consequences of the internet for politics. Annual Review of Political Science.

Fayyaz, S. (2018). A review on measuring digital trade & e-commerce as new economic statistics products. IAOS.

Feigenbaum, C. (2018, 11 12). Social Media Creating Political Change In Ethiopia. NATEBASE.

Feyisa, G. (2017, 04 17). Ethiopia's Population Growth-It's Consequence. Addis Fortun.

Fick, M. (2019, 06 24). Explainer: Ethiopia's ethnic militias in the spotlight after a failed coup. REUTERS.

Fidelis, M. (2019). Outrage over Ethiopia's continuing internet blackout. Aljazeera.

Foerster, B. (2019). The Amazing Megalithic Obelisks Of Axum In Ethiopia. Retrieved from Hidden Inc: https://hiddenincatours.com/the-amazing-megalithic-obelisks-of-axum-in-ethiopia/

Fong, M. W. (2017). Digital Divide: The Case of Developing Countries. Issues in Informing Science & Information Technology.

Fonseca, J. F. (2014). How sample size influences research outcomes. Dental Press Journal of Orthodontics, 1.

Fonseca, J. F. (2014). How sample size influences research outcomes. Dental Journal of Orthodontics.

Francesca, M. (2019). Digital Trade. ECIPE.

(2020). Freedom in the world 2020. Freedom House.

Fuchs, C. (2008). *Africa and the digital divide. Science Direct.*

Gallardo, R. (2018). *Research and Policy INsights: Digital Divide in the US. Prudent University.*

Ganesan, A. (2014). *Ethiopia: Telecom Surveillance Chills Rights. Human Rights Report.*

Gardner, T. (2020). *Will Abiy Ahmed's Bet on Ethiopia's Political Future Pay Off? FP.*

Gebreluel, G. (2019, April 15). *Should Ethiopia stick with ethnic federalism? African Opinion.*

Gedamu, Y. (2018). *How Ethiopia's history of ethnic rivalry is destabilizing its reform gains. Quartz Africa.*

Getachew, S. (2019, 06 17). *Ethiopia has been offline, and nobody knows why. CNN.*

Getachew, S. (2020). *The internet is back on in Ethiopia but there's every chance it'll be off again soon. Quartz Africa.*

Getachew, Y. Y. (2019, November 15). *Ethiopia's inability to protect its ethnic minorities is the biggest obstacle to peace. QUARTIZAFRICA.*

Ghaith Shennib, A. S. (2018). *Libya, Somalia raids show U.S. reach, problems. Returns.*

Ghedamu, T. (2020). *Ethiopian activist and singer buried as 81 killed in protests. CNN.*

Gilardi, F. (2016). *DIGITAL DEMOCRACY How Digital Technology Is Changing Democracy and Its Study. The University of Zurich.*

Giorgis, H. (2018). *Abiy Ahmed Meets the Ethiopian Diaspora. The Atlantic.*

Gizaw, S. (2020, 09 30). *Current Political Situation of Ethiopia in terms of Promoting Digital Marketing. (D. Solomon, Interviewer)*

Goitom, G. (2019). *Should Ethiopia stick with ethnic federalism? Africa.*

Gonzalez, M. (2019). *The Plot to Change America: How Identity Politics Is Dividing the Land of the Free. Amazon Books.*

Group, M. M. (2019, May 23). *Internet world stats. Retrieved from Ethiopia Internet Marketing, Search Engines and Telecommunications:* https://www.internetworldstats.com/africa.htm#et

Gunkel, D. (2003). Second thoughts: toward a critique of the digital divide. Journal of New Media & Society, 499–522.

Habas, C. (2018). How Has Technology Impacted the Global Business Environment? Bizfulent.

Hadingham, E. (2015). Where Is the Birthplace of Humankind? South Africa and East Africa Both Lay Claims. National Geography, 1.

Hailu, C. (2020, 2 5). Current Political Situation of Ethiopia in terms of Promoting Digital Marketing. (D. Solomon, Interviewer)

Hannah, R. (1998). The Emerging Significance of Internet Association. HeinOnline.

Hasani, N. (2015). ICT Impact in Fighting Corruption in Albania: New Ways in Increasing Transparency. Academic Journal of Interdisciplinary Studies.

Hibert. (2016). The bad news is that the digital access divide is here to stay: Domestically installed bandwidths among 172 countries for 1986. Science Direct.

Hill, D. a. (2005). The Internet in Indonesia's new democracy. New York: Routledge.

Hoover, N. E. (2019). Hooked: How to Build Habit-Forming Products. New York: Amazon Books.

How ethnic violence is destabilizing Ethiopia's reform gains. (2018, 10 1). The Conversation.

Howard, P. N. (2005). Deep Democracy, Thin Citizenship: The Impact of Digital Media in Political Campaign Strategy. AAPSS.

Hunter, R. (2014, 09 14). 40 Years Ago: Communist Coup Deposed Ethiopia's Last Emperor. Retrieved from The Institute of Religion and Democracy: https://juicyecumenism.com/2014/09/22/40-years-ago-communist-coup-deposed-ethiopias-last-emperor/

Hussain, W. (2012). E-learning: Closing the digital gap between Developed and Developing countries. Journal of Basic and Applied Sciences, 262.

ICG. (2019). Ethiopia: Ethnic Federalism and Its Discontents.

Infoplease. (2019). Ethiopia. Retrieved from Infoplease: https://www.infoplease.com/world/countries/ethiopia

(2020). Internet cut in Ethiopia. Netblock.

(2020). *Internet cut in Ethiopia amid unrest following the killing of the singer. ECADF.*

(2020). *Internet shutdown costs Ethiopia $100 million. TrendsNAfrica.*

Internet was used by 3.2 billion people in 2015, (2015, 5 26). Retrieved from BBC: www.bbc.com

(2017). *Internet Users Statistics for Africa. Miniwatts Marketing Groups.*

(2019). *Internet World Stats. Internet World Stats.*

Iqbal, M. (2020). *Facebook User Statistics. Business of Apps.*

ISI. (2018, 11 15). *Developing Countries. Retrieved from ISI: https:// isi-web.org/index.php/resources/developing-countries*

Itimu, K. (2019). *Internet Access in Ethiopia is Reportedly Cutoff Due to An Interesting Reason. Tecjweez.*

Jackson, J. J. (2018). *History of the Black Man: an authentic collection of historical information on the early civilization of the Descendents of Ham, the son of Noah. Amazon Books.*

Jaide, D. (2007). *The Black Gods: Ethiopia and the Origin of Civilization Part 4 – By John G. Jackson (1939). Rsta Livewire,* 1.

James, J. (2003). *Bridging the Global Digital Divide. Tilburg University, The Netherlands: EE Publishing.*

Jeffrey, J. (2018). *Ethnic Violence in Ethiopia Stoked by Social Media from U.S. IPS.*

Jeffrey, J. (2019, 02 22). *Social media users in America are stoking Ethiopia's ethnic violence. PRI.*

Jensen, R. (2007). *The digital provide Information (technology) market performance and welfare in the south Indian fisheries sector. The Quarterly Journal of Economics,*

Jiwa, B. (2016). *Marketing: A Love Story: How to Matter to Your Customers. New York: Amazon Books.*

Jiwa, B. (2016). *Marketing: A Love Story: How to Matter to Your Customers. New York.*

John, V. (2019). *The Digital Divide and Factors affecting Global Digital Divide. Greek.*

Kaigo, M. (2002). *Cultural Factors Affecting Digital Skills and the Digital Divide in Japan. Presented at the 23rd International*

Association for Media and Communication Research. Barcelona: University of Tsukuba.

Kajornboon, A. B. (2005). Using interviews as research instruments. E-Journal for Researching Teachers (EJRT).

Kajornboon, A. B. (2005). Using interviews as research instruments. E-Journal for Researching Teachers (EJRT).

Kallmer, J. (. (2019). The United States is Poised to Lead on Digital Trade. TechWonk.

Kaplan, K. (2015, 10 05). DNA from 4,500year-old Ethiopian reveals surprise about the ancestry of Africans. Los Angelse Times, p. 1.

Katherine, S. (2010). Digital marketing strategies that Millennials find appealing, motivating, or just annoying. Journal of Strategic Marketing.

Kauffman, R. B. (2017). Integrated Risk Management for Leisure Services First Edition. Amazon Book Clubs.

Kaur, K. K. (2016). Pay-per-click advertising: A literature review. Westburn Publishers Ltd.

Kaveh, W. (2016, Sept 6). The Internet May Be as Segregated as a City. Retrieved from The Atlantic: https://www.theatlantic.com/technology/archive/2016/09/the-internet-may-be-as-segregated-as-a-city/498608/

Keith, M. C. (2019). Place and the Politics of Identity. Amazon Books.

Kelecha, M. (2018). Protest, Repression, and Revolution in Ethiopia. African Political Economy.

KEMP, S. (2019, 01 30). DIGITAL 2019: GLOBAL INTERNET USE ACCELERATES. Retrieved from We are Social: https://wearesocial.com/blog/2019/01/digital-2019-global-internet-use-accelerates

Keniston, K. (2003). The Four Digital Divides. Delhi.

Kiani, G. R. (2020). Marketing opportunities in the digital world. Emerald Insight.

Kingsnorth, S. (2019). Digital Marketing Strategy: An Integrated Approach to Online Marketing. Amazon Books.

Kingsnorth, S. (2019). Digital Marketing Strategy: An Integrated Approach to Online Marketing. New York.

Kingsnorth, S. (2020). *Digital Marketing Strategy: An Integrated Approach to Online Marketing 2nd Edition. Buzy Books.*

Klein, E. (2014). *Technology is changing how we live, but it needs to change how we work. Vox*

Kline, D. B. (2020). *How Many Customers Does Amazon Have? New York: The Motty Fool.*

KUMAR, M. A. (2019, May 7). *The digital divide persists even as lower-income Americans make gains in tech adoption. Fact Thank.*

Kuo, J.-H. (2011). *Ten Years of Digital Divide Studies: Themes, concepts, and relationships. Chang Jung Christian University.*

Kuyoro Shade O, O. S. (2012). *ICT: An Effective Tool in Human Development. Babcock University.*

Lajevardi, A. (2016). *Digitization of business is eliminating global trade barriers for SMBs. Tread Ready.*

Lambert, T. (2019). *A BRIEF HISTORY OF ETHIOPIA.*

LAROK, A. (2019, October 24). *Modified Activism After Ethiopia's New Dawn. CARNEGIE.*

Latif, D. A. (2017, 12 15). *Ethiopia has blocked social media sites as new Oromo protests hit the country. Quartz Africa.*

Leetaru, K. (2020). *Governments Can't Regulate Social Media Because They Are Too Dependent On It. Forbe.*

Lema, R. (2019, 01). *Availability, affordability, and accessibility of the Internet in Ethiopia. (D. Solomon, Interviewer)*

Lentz, R. &. (2002). *Digital divide or digital opportunity in the Mississippi Delta region of the US. Telecommunications Policy.*

Lewis, M. W. (2018). *Religious Change and Tension in Ethiopia. GeoCurrents, 1.*

Lin, Y. (2020). *10 EBAY STATISTICS. New York: OBERLO.*

Liu, Y. (2019). *Research on Digital Marketing Strategies of Fast Fashion Clothing Brands Based on Big Data. IEEE.*

lJoelJärvinen. (2015). *The use of Web analytics for digital marketing performance measurement. Science Direct.*

Lovise, A. (2011). *The politics of ethnicity in Ethiopia: Actors. power and mobilization under ethnic federalism. CMI.*

147

Lovise, A. (2011). *The politics of ethnicity in Ethiopia: Actors. power and mobilization under ethnic federalism. CMI.*

Lynch, K. (2019). *History of International Trade: Technology.*

Maasho, A. (2018). *At least 23 die during the weekend of Ethiopian ethnic violence. Returns.*

Mahmood, M. (2019, 01 03). *The Trouble With Ethiopia's Ethnic Federalism. The New York Times.*

Mamdani, M. (2019). *the current political canon, in-country, has put in place a legal framework in the form of a constitution that fragmented the country into nine regional states based on the ethnic sketches of the residents. The Washington Post.*

Mandel, M. (2017). *How Ecommerce Creates Jobs and Reduces Income Inequality. Progressive Policy Institute.*

Marcus, H. G. (1995). *The Life and Times of Menelik II: Ethiopia 1844-1913. In H. G. Marcus, The Life and Times of Menelik II: Ethiopia 1844-1913. (p. 241). Lawrenceville: Red Sea Press.*

Marmer, M. (2018, 02 12). *A Look at How Technology is Reshaping the Global Economy. Retrieved from https://medium.com/@maxmarmer/a-look-at-how-technology-is-reshaping-the-global-economy-c716c4681e06*

Martin, N. (2019). *Identity, Interest, and Ideology: An Introduction to Politics. Thriftbooks.*

Maryam, M. (2020). *10 ONLINE SHOPPING. Oberol.*

Matfess, H. (2019). *Ethno-regional divisions might tear apart hopes of unifying power at the center. EP.*

Mbah, F. (2009, 6 5). *Outrage over Ethiopia's continuing internet blackout.*

McCall, M. (2019). *The Swing Trader's Bible: Strategies to Profit from Market Volatility by Matthew McCall.*

McCombes, S. (2019). *How to write a literature review. Scribbler.*

Mebewa, D. (2020). *Ethiopia lost at least $100 million during the internet shutdown, a civil society group says. CGTN Africa.*

Mengisteab, K. (2018). *Ethnicity and Recent Democratic Experiments in Africa. Cambridge University Press, 20.*

Menu, A. (2008). *Age of New Media Empires: A Critical Interpretation of the Korean Online Game Industry.* SAGE.

Mercer, K. (2007). *Examining the impact of health information networks on health system integration in Canada. Leadership in Health Services, 43.*

Meredith, M. (2005). *The Fate of Africa: A History of Fifty Years of Independence.* New York: Public Affairs Publishing.

Mersha, M. (2019, 01 12). *Availability, affordability, and accessibility of the Internet in Ethiopia.* (D. Solomon, Interviewer)

Mickoleit, T. R. (2011). *The Economic Impact of Shutting Down Internet and Mobile Phone Services in Egypt. Organization for Economic Development and Cooperation.*

Miller, K. D. (1992). *A Framework for Integrated Risk Management in International Business. Journal of International Business.*

Milner, H. V. (2006). *The Digital Divide: The Role of Political Institutions in Technology Diffusion. SAGE Journals, 3.*

Min, S.-J. (2010, 02 01). *From the Digital Divide to the Democratic Divide: Internet Skills, Political Interest, and the Second-Level Digital Divide in Political Internet Use. Information Technology Politics, p. 23.*

Monette, D. (2013). *Applied Social Research (8th Ed). Phoenix: University of Phoenix.*

Moore, J. (2018). *Ethiopia's Prime Minister Resigns Amid Political Turmoil. The Washington Post.*

Mouton, S. H. (1987). *Mouton, S.G., Hawkins, J. McPherson, R.H.School Attachment: Perspectives of Low-Attached High School Students. Educational Psychology, Vol.16No. 3, pp.297-3(013987).*

MT. (2019). *Politics In These 3 African Countries Is Heavy. HowAfrica.*

Mulugeta, T. (2017, 02 17). *Ethiopia: The Ethiopian flag a symbol of unity. Retrieved from naZRET.COM: https://www.nazret. com/2017/02/18/ethiopia-the-ethiopian-flag-as-symbol-of-unity/*

Mumo, M. (2019). *In the era of reform, Ethiopia still reverts to old tactics to censor the press. CPJ.*

Mundi, I. (2017). *Ethiopia Demographic profile. Index Mundi.*

Muthoki, M. (2019). *In the era of reform, Ethiopia still reverts to old tactics to censor the press. CPJ.*

Nagy, T. P. (2020, 03 12). *TPLF started the Conflict 'to Depose Prime Minister from Power', Alludes U.S. Official. (E. Monitor, Interviewer) Ethiopian Monitor.*

Nayak, B. K. (2010). *Understanding the relevance of sample size calculation. Indian Journal of Ophthalmology.*

Negririo, M. (2015). *Bringing the Digital Divide to the EU. EPRS.*

Norries, P. (2009). *Digital Divide: Civic Engagement, Information Poverty and the Internet worldwide. Cambridge University.*

Norris, P. (2017). *Driving Democracy: Do Power-Sharing Institutions Work? Cambridge University Press.*

O.Nyumba, T. (2018). *The use of focus group discussion methodology: Insights from two decades of application in conservation. British Ecology Society.*

O'Leary, A. (2004). *The Essential Guide to Doing Research. London:: SAGE Publications.*

Oak, M. (2018, 02 28). *What is the Impact of Technology on Our Society? A Critical Analysis. Retrieved from TechSprited: https://techspirited.com/what-is-impact-of-technology-on-our-society*

Oberski, I. (2004). *University continuing education: The role of communications and information technology. Journal of European Industrial Training, 414.*

Ochieng, R. O. (2000). *Library Management Journal. Global information flows 14.*

Ott, D. a. (2000). *The electronic republic? The role of the Internet in promoting democracy in Africa.*

P.K.Kannan. (2017). *Digital marketing: A framework, review, and research agenda. Science Direct.*

Pandey, N. (2020). *Digital marketing for B2B organizations: structured literature review and future research directions. Emerald Insight.*

Parayil, G. (2007). *The Digital Divide and Increasing Return: Contradictions of Informational Capitalism. The Information Society.*

Pardeshi, G. S. (2010). *Age Heaping and Accuracy of Age Data Collected During a Community Survey in the Yavatmal District, Maharashtra. Indian J Community Med.*

Park, H. (2018). *Internet effects on political participation: Digital Divide, causality, and new Digital Divide. Purdue University.*

Parvez, S. J. (2016). *Digital marketing in the hotel industry. International Journal of Engineering & Technology.*

Pathmalal, L. (2013, 03 26). *Why ICT (Information and Communication Technologies) and why NOW? Retrieved from World Bank: http:// blogs.worldbank.org/endpovertyinsouthasia/why-ict-information-and-communication-technologies-and-why-now*

Paul. (2014, 10 14). *In Ethiopia's war against social media, the truth is the main casualty. The Washington Post.*

Paul, S. (2016, 10 14). *In Ethiopia's war against social media, the truth is the main casualty. Retrieved from worldview: https:// www.washingtonpost.com/news/worldviews/wp/2016/10/14/ in-ethiopias-war-against-social-media-the-truth-is-the-main-casualty/?utm_term=.35303ba67ea1*

Perrin, A. &. (2015). *Americans' Internet Access: 2000-2015. Pew Research Center.*

Picincu, A. (2018). *The Advantages of Using ICT. Bisukent.*

Pilling, D. (2018). *Ethnic clashes in Ethiopia leave at least 80 dead. Financial Times.*

Pillow, A. (2020). *School Districts Are Not Equipped to Close the Digital Divide. INDY K12.*

Primary data and secondary data. (2019). *Institute for work and health.*

radio, o. (2006, 12 6). *How radio, cell phones, wireless web are empowering developing nations. Retrieved from http://radio. oneworld.net/article/view/78640/1*

Rainie, J. A. (2018). *Concerns about the future of people's well-being. Internet and Technology.*

Rainie, L. (2010). *Internet, broadband, and cell phone statistics. PewInternet.*

(2021). *Rapid development and popularization of the Internet. UKEssays.*

Rapid Development of Information Technology in the 20th Century. (2019). Retrieved from United Nations: file:///C:/Users/Lenovo/ Downloads/Part1_68335.pdf

Raugh, H. E. (2014). *The Victorians at War, 1815–1914: An Encyclopedia of British Military History. In H. E. Raugh. ABC-CLIO.*

Reda, Y. (2018). *E-marketing for Tourism Business Development in Ethiopia: Its Practice, Challenges, and Implications on Performance of Tour Operating Firms. AAU.*

Redding, R. (2020). *The Book On Digital Marketing. HippieCow.*

Review. (2019, 07 26). *Making Sense of the Digital Divide: Literature Review. Retrieved from Review: https://newsflash.one/2019/02/12/ making-sense-of-the-digital-divide-literature-review/*

Rheingold, H. (1993). *The virtual community: Homesteading on the electronic frontier. New York.*

Riggins, F. J. (2005). *The Digital Divide: Current and Future Research Directions. Journal of the Association for Information Systems.*

Rouse, M. (2019). *Digital Divide. TechTarget.*

Royle, l. (2014). *The digital marketing skills gap: Developing a Digital Marketer Model for the communication industries. Science Direct.*

Rrostcki, N. (2020). *The role of information and communication technologies in socio-economic development: towards a multi-dimensional framework. Journal of Information Technology for Development.*

Ryan. (2019). *Hooked: How to Build Habit-Forming Products. New York: Amazon Books.*

Ryan, D. (2018). *Digital Marketing For Dummies, 2nd Edition. New York: Amazon Books.*

S, S. (2018, 07 25). *Difference Between Developed Countries and Developing Countries. Retrieved from Key Differences: https:// keydifferences.com/difference-between-developed-countries-and-developing-countries.html*

Saini, S. (2018). *11 Benefits of Digital Marketing over Traditional Marketing. Technical.*

Samuel D. (2014). *Internet Research in Psychology.* AR.

San, M.-c. L. (2006, 04 21). *Social Learning and Digital Divide: A Case Study of Internet Technology Diffusion.* Wiley Online Library.

San, M.-c. L. (2018). *Social Learning and Digital Divide: A Case Study of Internet Technology Diffusion.* The University of Tasmania.

Sani, A. (2017). *Issue s in Informing Science and Information Technology Digital Divide: The Case of Developing Countries.* Academia.

Sani, G. (2019). *Sex and Gender Equity in Research: rationale for the SAGER guidelines and recommended use.* NCBI.

Saura, J. R. (2017). *Understanding the Digital Marketing Environment with KPIs and Web Analytics.* MDPI.

Saura, J. R. (2018). *Digital Marketing Strategies Based on the E-Business Model: Literature Review and Future Directions.* IGI Global.

Schmutzer, G. A. (2001). *The Digital Divide in Austria.* Institute of Technology Assessment.

Selwyn, N. (2001). *Defining the 'Digital Divide': Developing a Theoretical Understanding of Inequalities in the Information Age.* Cardiff University - School of Social Sciences.

Shaban, A. R. (2019). *Social media helped 'topple' repressive Ethiopian regime – Top journalist.* African news.

(2020). *Shaping our future together.* United Nations.

Sharziz, F. (2014). *ICT expansion and the digital divide in democratic freedoms: An analysis of the impact of ICT expansion, education and ICT filtering on democracy.* Science Direct.

Shelley, M. C. (2006). *Lost in cyberspace: barriers to bridging the digital divide in e-politics.* Management, International Journal of Internet and Enterprise, 23.

Sherman. (2019). *Digital Marketing vs Traditional Marketing: Which Produces Better ROI?* LYFE.

ShihuiFeng. (2019). *The Internet and Facebook Usage on Academic Distraction of College Students.* Computer and Education.

Shillington, V. G. (2017). *James and Paul: The Politics of Identity at the Turn of the Ages.* Amazon Books.

Shull, D. (2012). *Market Mind Games: A Radical Psychology of Investing, Trading, and Risk.*

Simon, K. (2019). *Digital Marketing Strategy: An Integrated Approach to Online Marketing. New York: Amazon Books.*

Simon, K. (2020). *DIGITAL 2020: ETHIOPIA. Data portal.*

Smith, A. (2014). *Older Adults and Technology Use. Internet and Thecnology.*

Snyder, I. (2013). *Beyond the 'Digital Divide' Engaging with New Technologies in Marginalised Educational Settings in Australia. Monash University.*

Social Media Stats Kenya. (2019, May). *Retrieved from Understand your visitors with Statcounter: http://gs.statcounter.com/social-media-stats/all/kenya*

Solomon, S. (2017). *As Violence Flares in Ethiopia, Internet Goes Dark. VOA.*

Solomon, S. (2018, October 3). *VOA News. Retrieved from https://www.voanews.com/africa/when-violence-flares-ethiopia-continues-turn-internet*

Srihari, V. (2016). *Digital divide Definition and usage. Academia.*

Steenbarger, B. N. (2015). *Trading Psychology 2.0: From Best Practices to Best Processes.*

Stefen, E. (2018). *Why Manufacturing Digitalization Matters and How Countries Are Supporting It. ITIF.*

Sullivan, K. (2019, 4 13). *The Kingdom of Axum: Facts and Legends of a First Millennium Powerhouse. Retrieved from https://www.ancient-origins.net/ancient-places-africa/axum-legendary-kingdom-ancient-ethiopia-006720*

(2008). *Summary and Statistical Report of the 2007 Population and Housing Census Results. Central Statistical Agency.*

Sun, J. C.-Y. (2011). *The Digital Divide and Its Impact on Academic Performance. National Chiao Tung University.*

Suzuki, L. (2015, 09 11). *The Digital Divide: Bridge that Gap! Retrieved from OpenSeSame: https://www.opensesame.com/site/blog/digital-divide-bridge-gap/*

Suzuki, L. (2015, Sept 12). *The Digital Divide: Bridge that Gap! Retrieved from OpenSesame: https://www.opensesame.com/site/blog/digital-divide-bridge-gap/*

T Stephen, A. (2016). The role of digital and social media marketing in consumer behavior. ScienceDirect, 21.

Taye, B. A. (2019). Ethnic federalism and conflict in Ethiopia. ACCORD.

Taye, D. B. (2017). Ethnic federalism and conflict in Ethiopia. Accord.

Taylor, E. (2018). Bridging the Digital Divide: infrastructure, skills and women's empowerment. G20.

Tekelab, T. (2015). Predictors of modern contraceptive methods use among married women of reproductive age groups in Western Ethiopia: a community-based cross-sectional study. PMC.

Tekle, F. (2019). Ethiopia: Lack of accountability for past violations haunts the present. Amnesty International.

(2014). Telecom and Internet Surveillance in Ethiopia. Human Rights Watch.

Tesfaye, A. (2018). COMMENTARY: THE BIRTH OF AMHARA NATIONALISM: CAUSES, ASPIRATIONS, AND POTENTIAL IMPACTS. Addis Standard.

Thakur, M. (2020). Country Risk. Wellsfargo.

(2016). The economic impact of disruptions to Internet connectivity. Facebook.

(2016). The economic impact of disruptions to Internet connectivity. Deloitte.

(2020). The Ethiopian government must end internet shutdowns to quell protests. keeping.

Thomas, R. (2019). Identity Politics at Work: Resisting Gender, Gendering Resistance. Thriftbooks.

Tim, L. (2019). A BRIEF HISTORY OF ETHIOPIA. Retrieved from localhistory.org: http://www.localhistories.org/ethiopia.html

Tobor, N. (2017, 6 1). Ethiopia's Authorities Have Shut Down The Internet Without Giving Any Reasons. African.

Toksöz, M. (2014). Guide to Country Risk: How to identify, manage and mitigate the risks of doing business across borders (Economist Books) Paperback – Illustrated.

(2019). Total internet outage identified in Ethiopia. Netblocks.

Tronvoll, K. (2019). The End of Democracy? Curtailing Political and Civil Rights in Ethiopia. Journal of the University of Oslo.

Turton, D. (2016). *Four Questions about Ethiopia's Ethnic Federalism. St. Antony's International Review.*

Understanding the Digital Divide. (2010). Retrieved from Learn.org: https://learn.org/articles/Understanding_the_Digital_Divide.html

van Dijk, J. a. (2002). *The 'Digital Divide' as a Complex and Dynamic Phenomenon. The Information Society.*

Varghese, A. (2017, May 18). *Experience in digital marketing.* Retrieved from QUADRA: https://www.quora.com/Which-country-uses-digital-marketing-the-most

Voas, D. (2007). *Does Religion Belong in Population Studies? SAGE Journals.*

Vostrikova, A. (2014). *The Importance of Data on the Age and Sex Structure of the Population. Journal of Problems in Economics.*

Wagner, D. (2016). *Managing Country Risk. Taylor & Francis.*

Warschauer, M. (2004). *Technology and Social Inclusion. Cambridge.*

Warschauer, M. (2020). *Technology and Social Inclusion: Rethinking the Digital Divide. Amazon.*

Warshauer, M. (2019). *Reconceptualzing the digital divde. Journal of the internet.*

Wharton. (2019). *The bad news is that the digital access divide is here to stay: Domestically installed bandwidths among 172 countries for 1986. The Wharton School.*

(2020). *What Is Internet Surveillance and How to Avoid It? CatusVPN.*

Wiener, J. B. (2018, 06 13). *Information & Communication Technologies in Cultural Heritage & Tourism.* Retrieved from Ancient History: https://www.ancient.eu/article/1242/information--communication-technologies-in-cultura/

Wilsson, T. (2019, 05 30). *Ethnic violence in Ethiopia has forced nearly 3 million people from their homes. Financial Times.*

Woodhams. (2019). *Ethiopia's leader promised to protect freedom of expression. But he keeps flicking the internet kill switch. CNN.*

Woods, J. (2020). *Protest against the Ethiopian government takes over the Downtown intersection. The Wahington Post.*

world, C. o. (2019, 02 09). Ethiopian People 2019. Retrieved from Countries of the world: https://www.theodora.com/wfbcurrent/ethiopia/ethiopia_people.html

world, H. (2019). The kingdom of Aksum: from the 5ᵗʰ century BC. Retrieved from History of the world: http://www.historyworld.net/wrldhis/PlainTextHistories.asp?groupid=2112&HistoryID=ab92&gtrack=pthc

Worldmeters. (2019, 07 24). Ethiopia Population. Worldmeters.

WPT, J. (2012, 09 28). How ICT changed the world! Retrieved from https://prezi.com/q0wipfqajt3p/how-ict-changed-the-world/

WTO. (2017, 11 30). Debating the Future of E-Commerce and Digital Trade in Buenos Aires. Retrieved from BRIDGES: Estimates published by eMarketer, a news and research site on digital trends, put global e-commerce website sales at above US\$22 trillion last year, with projections that they will expand to US\$27 trillion by 2020.

Wymbs, C. (2011). Digital Marketing: The Time for a New "Academic Major" Has Arrived. Journal of Marketing Education.

Yi, X. (2018). The 2018 World Trade Report 2018. World Trade Organzation.

Zewde, B. (2001). A History of Modern Ethiopia (second ed.). Oxford: James Currey.

Zimmerman, J. (2017). Social Media Marketing All-in-One. New York: Amazon Books.

Appendix 1:
The Research Proposal

Dissertation Thesis Proposal

Name of student:

Daniel Solomon

Title:

Identity Politics and Its Impact on the Spread of Digital Marketing (A Framework to Manage Country Level Political Risk in Ethiopia)

Topic:

As indicated above the topic of the research is "Identity Politics and Its Impact on the Spread of Digital Marketing (A Framework to Manage Country Level Political Risk in Ethiopia)". In this modern world, digital marketing has a significant contribution to economic growth (Redding, 2020). Public passion is essentials for sustaining effective digital marketing (Kingsnorth, Digital Marketing Strategy: An Integrated Approach to Online Marketing 2nd Edition, 2020). Countries led by a political ideology that risks the prevalence of such a passion do not give the impression to benefit from digital marketing. Instead, the digital divide is becoming an imminent danger that they might encounter (Mark, 2020). This Study centers on Ethiopia, a country once signified as the cradle of mankind with a civilization of over 3000 years (Jackson, 2018) and now at the threshold of collapsing due to identity politics (Bahru, 2018), it has been adhered to, for the last thirty years (Berhe, 2016).

Research Goals and Questions:

The purpose of the research is to find out if identity politics has a significant relationship with the public passion for digital marketing. The research addresses four questions: 1) Does identity politics have a significant relationship with the public passion for digital marketing? 2) Will identity politics lead to a digital divide? 3) Why is identity politics considered a country-level political risk for Ethiopia? 4) What kind of risk management framework would best help Ethiopia to reverse the course of the problem?

Key Points:

The research will have five main chapters: 1) Introduction, 2) Review of related literature, 3) Methodology 4) Discussion and findings, 5) Conclusion and recommendation

Research Methodology:

The research hypothesizes identity politics, which is presumed as a country-level risk in this research, has a significant relationship with public passion for doing digital marketing. They are inversely proportional. In other words, the intensification of the former causes the redaction and/or obliteration of the latter. The null hypothesis, on the other hand, the aforementioned variables have no substantial association. Review of related literature and questionnaire, focused group discussion, and interview will be used to collect both quantitative and qualitative data. GPower will be used to define a statistically sound and representative sample size population. Informants will be selected randomly with qualifying criteria, which include age, academic level, and passion for digital marketing. Using JAMOVIA, the collected data will be analyzed and synthesized to address the research questions.

Significance of Thesis:

The ever-growing consumption of digital marketing is being perceived as the most important factor to reinforce the social and economic development of any given society at any corner of the world (Selwyn, 2001). This research will highlight the roadblocks for the expansion of digital marketing in Ethiopia along with its possible solutions. Hence, the concerned stakeholders will use the findings of the research to make an informed decision on their efforts concerning digital marketing.,

Bibliography

Bahru, Z. (2018). *A History of Modern Ethiopia, 1855-1991.* thrift books.

Bedasso, G. G. (2018, 02 07). Managing Ethiopia's political crisis. *Opinion Africa.*

Berhe, M. g. (2016). *Laying the Past to Rest: The EPRDF and the Challenges of Ethiopian State: New.*

Farrell, H. (2012). The consequences of the internet for politics. *Annual Review of Political Science.*

Getachew, S. (2019, 06 17). Ethiopia has been offline, and nobody knows why. *CNN.*

Kingsnorth, S. (2020). *Digital Marketing Strategy: An Integrated Approach to Online Marketing 2nd Edition.* Buzy Books.

Lambert, T. (2019). *A BRIEF HISTORY OF ETHIOPIA.*

Lynch, K. (2019). *History of International Trade: Technology.*

Mamdani, M. (2019, 01 03). The Trouble With Ethiopia's Ethnic Federalism. *The New York Times.*

Norris, P. (2017). *Driving Democracy: Do Power-Sharing Institutions Work?* Cambridge University Press.

Redding, R. (2020). *The Book On Digital Marketing.* HippieCow.

Rouse, M. (2019). Digital Divide. *TechTarget.*

Schemm, P. (2014, 10 14). In Ethiopia's war against social media, the truth is the main casualty. *The Washington Post.*

Solomon, S. (2018, October 3). *VOA News.* Retrieved from https://www.voanews.com/africa/when-violence-flares-ethiopia-continues-turn-internet

WILSON, T. (2019, 05 30). Ethnic violence in Ethiopia has forced nearly 3 million people from their homes. *Financial Times.*

About the Author

DANIEL B. SOLOMON IS A naturalized citizen of the United States of America with Ethiopian background. He is a multi-professional expert practicing in literature, software engineering, project management, and leadership.

Solomon is a part-time novelist and poet writing both in English and Amharic, the official vernacular language of the Democratic Republic of Ethiopia. Some of his published books include Abeshatay, Tachyon, Blue Wave, The Sold Nation, The War of Two Brothers, and Africa Distracted. The first two are novels, text in Amharic. The third and the fourth books are also novels, written in English, while the last two are collections of poems, written in English.

Identity Politics and Its Impact on the Spread of Digital Marketing (A Framework to Manage Country Level Political Risk in Ethiopia) is a research work made for the partial fulfillment of a PhD degree in Project Management at LIGS University, which is located at 810 Richards St, Honolulu, HI 96813 USA. The research work is supervised by Professor George Alexander and approved by other two opponent professors.

"The Impact of Tribal Politics on Public Passion to Digital Trade in Current Ethiopia", "The Worth of Steady Digital Team Formation Strategy: A Case Study of Bruce Tuckman's Model in Software Industry", "The Worth of SWOT in Digital Sales Planning", "Practical Returns of Agile Project Management Model (APM)" and "The Inference of Transparency in Effective Team Management" are some of his published articles in scientific journals such as Advanced Journal of Social Science and Humanities, International Journal of Innovative Research in Information Securities, and Journal of Computer Science and Engineering.

Printed in the United States
by Baker & Taylor Publisher Services